I0461778

The word 'mantra' means circle in Sanskrit, a symbol to represent the universe. Modern interpretation of the word also may now include any circular pattern, diagram, or geometric repetition. There are many resources available if you wish to research further regarding mandalas, patterns, symbols, and rituals.

The purpose of this book is to enjoy colouring the images, relax, and allow your creativity to flow. You are welcome to also play music in the background, diffuse or wear essential oils, or have another tool to assist with holding your preferred ambience. This book may be used by yourself, or as a facilitated group activity for circles, retreats, and other similar sessions.

Thank you for purchasing this book, and I would love to hear from you your experience of using Colouring Mantras.

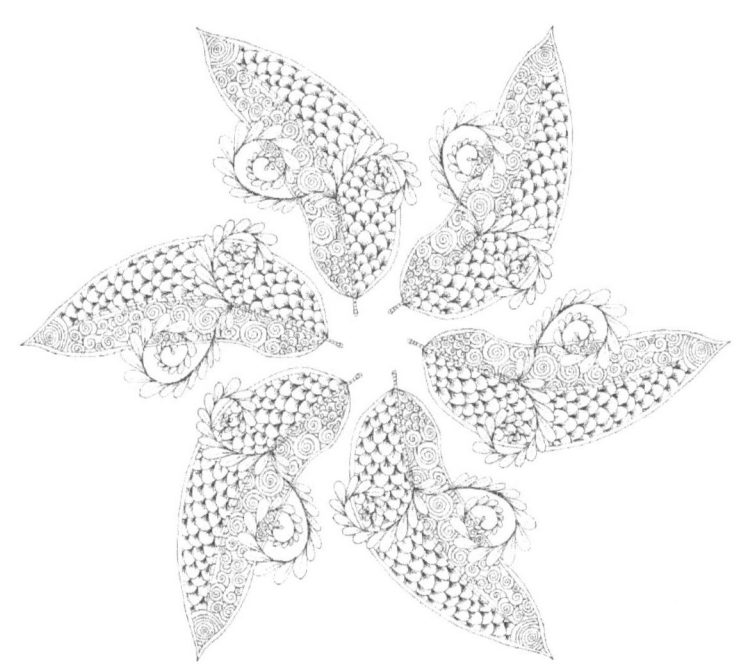

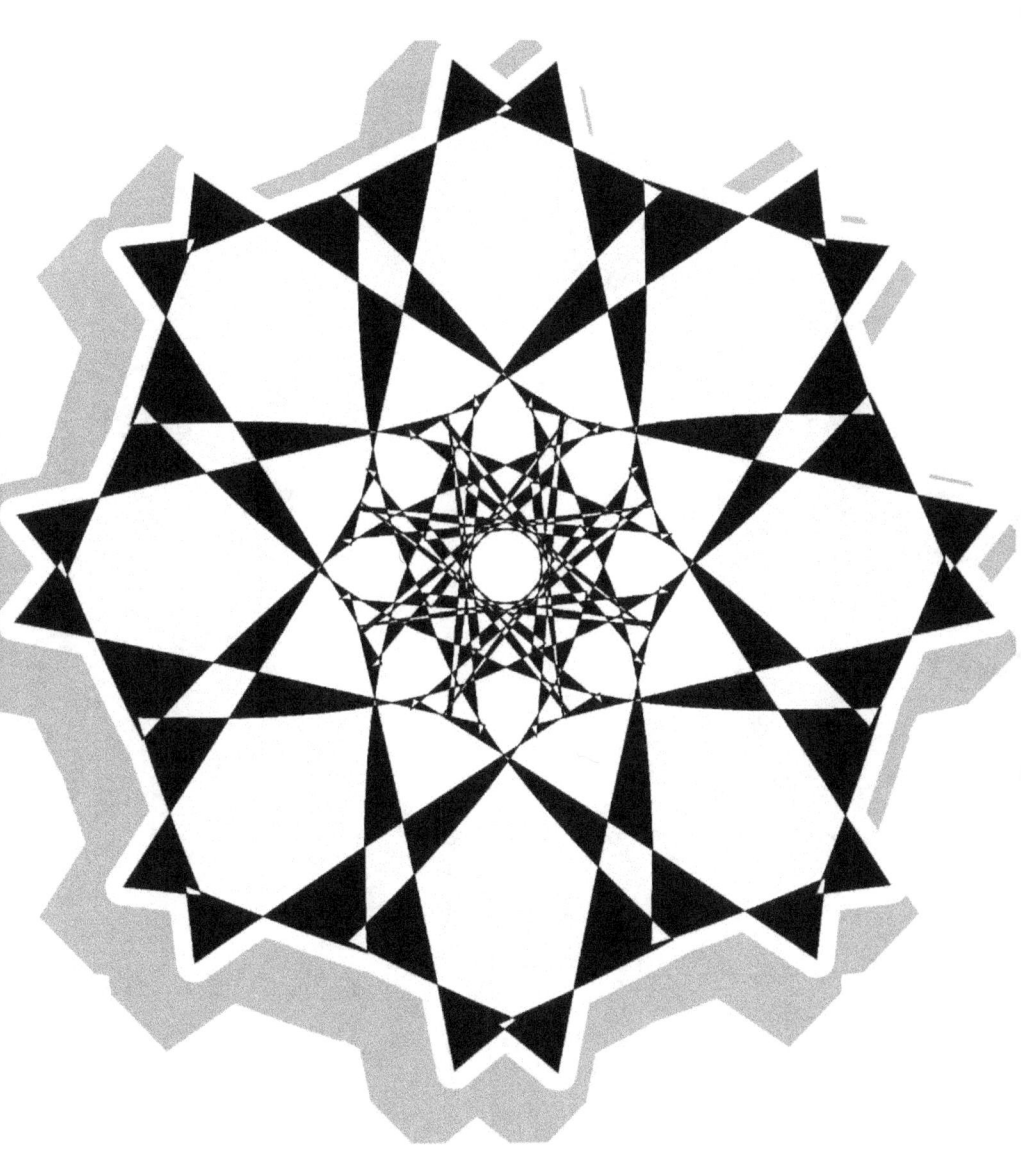

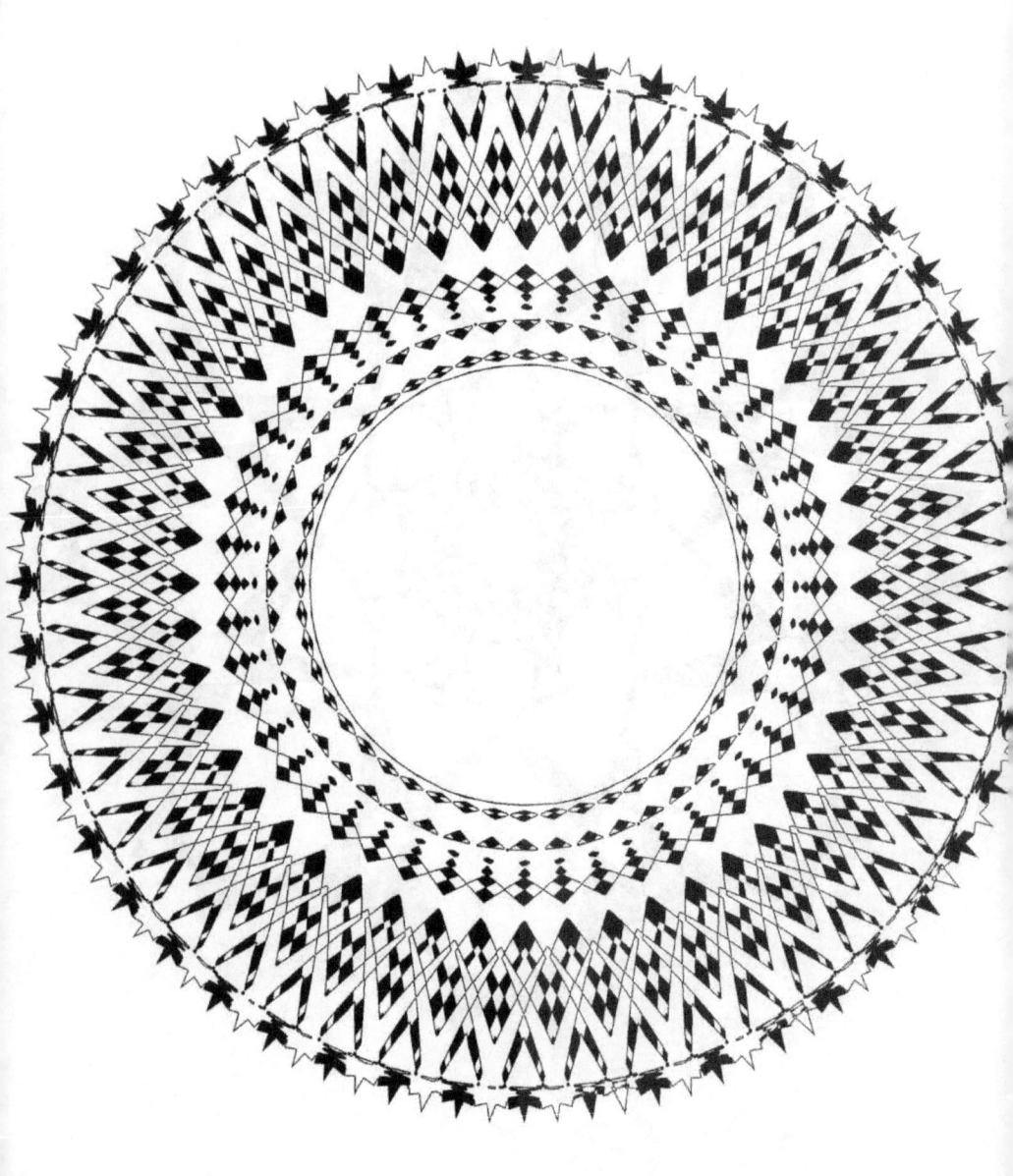

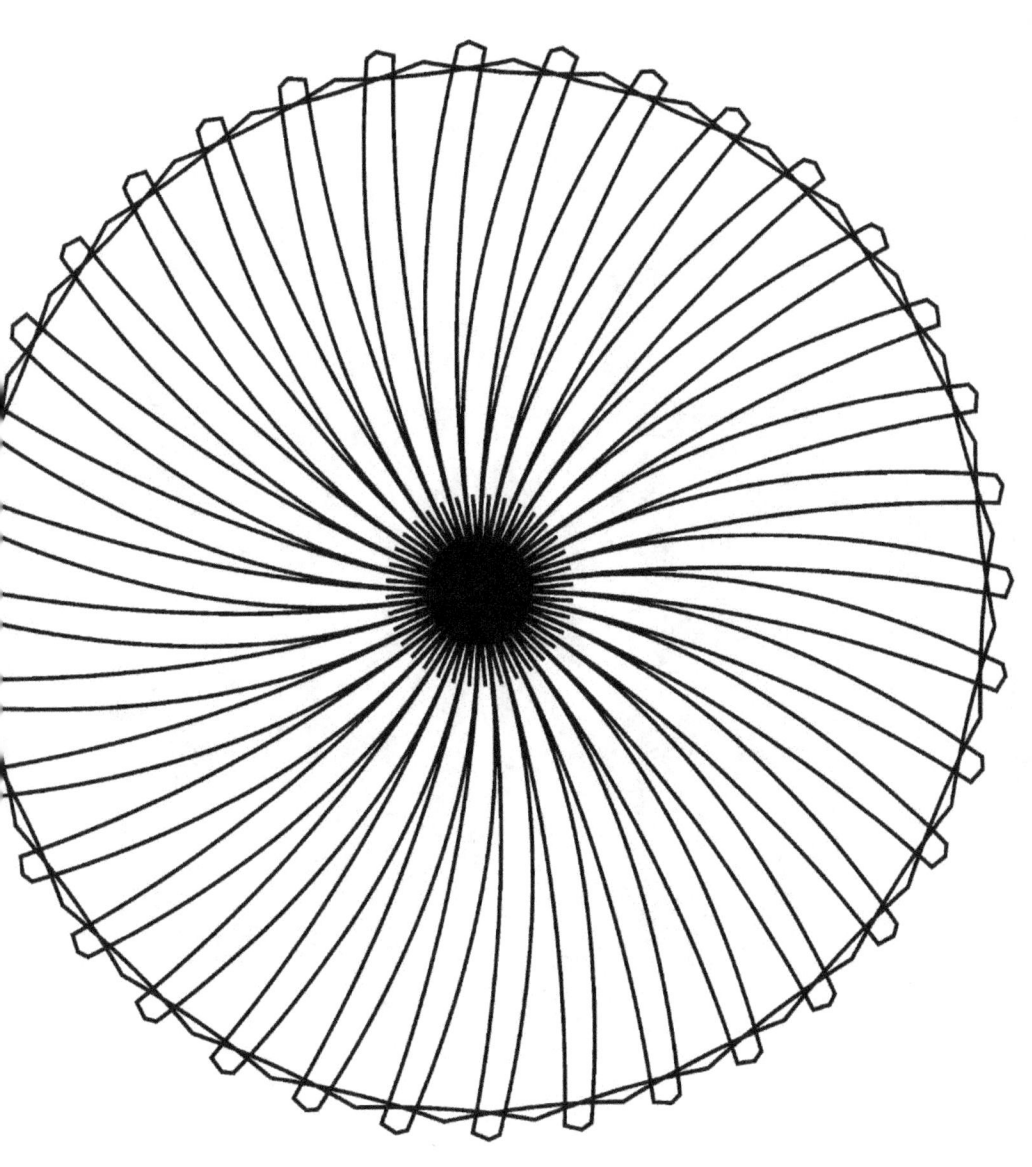

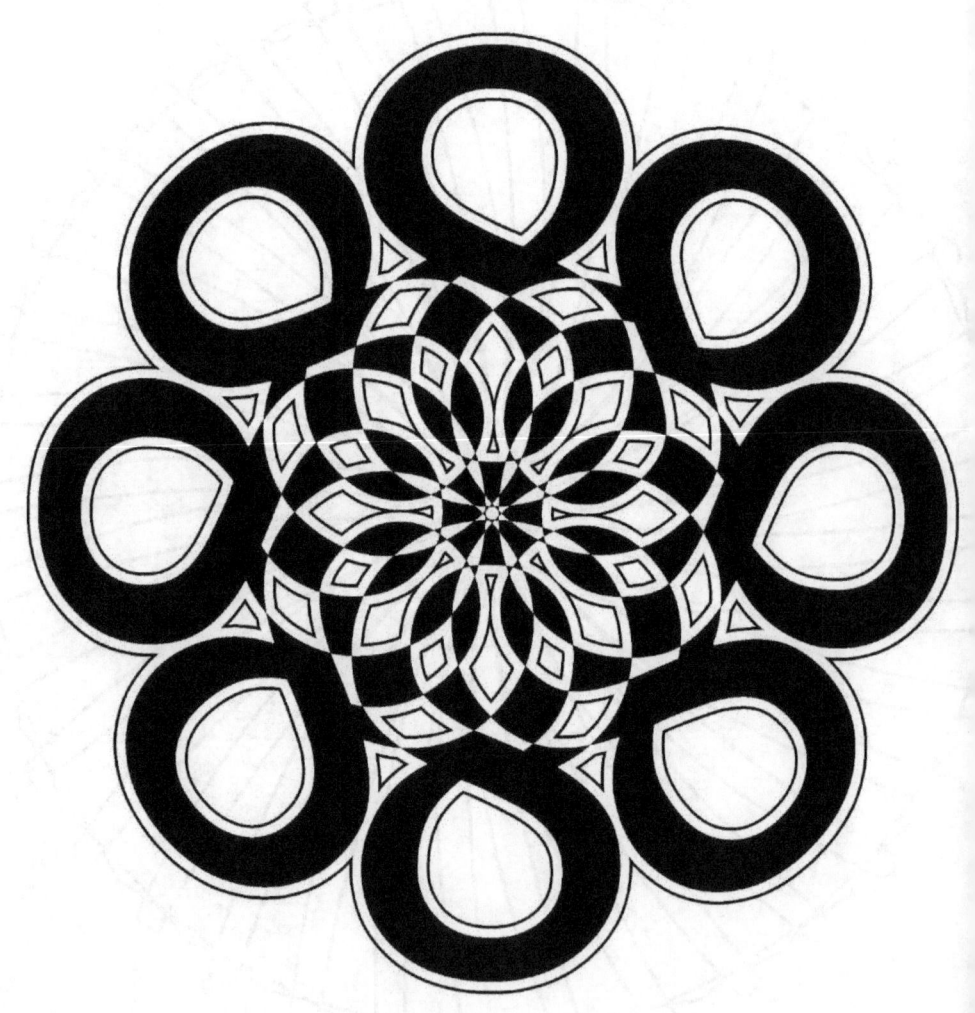

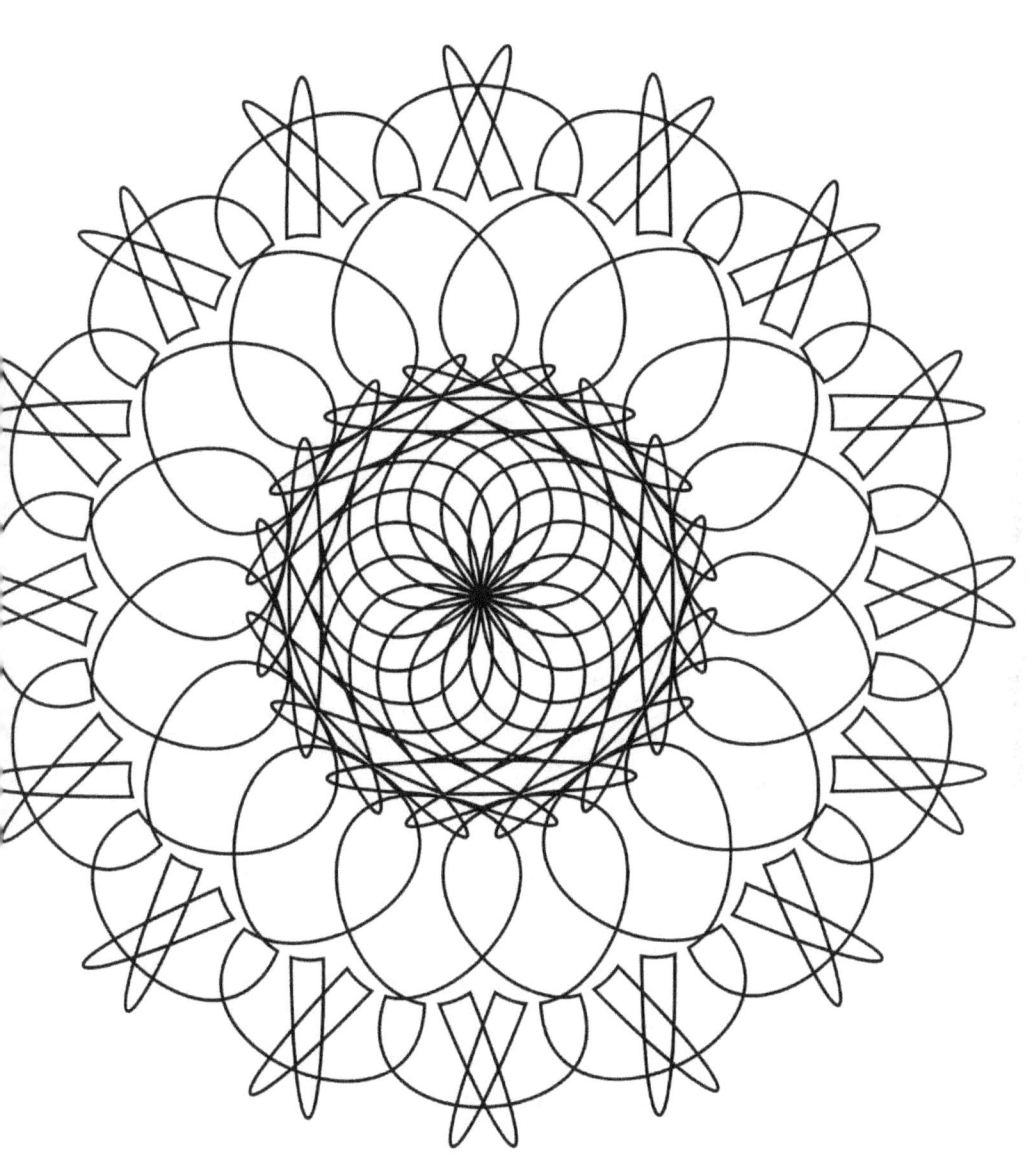

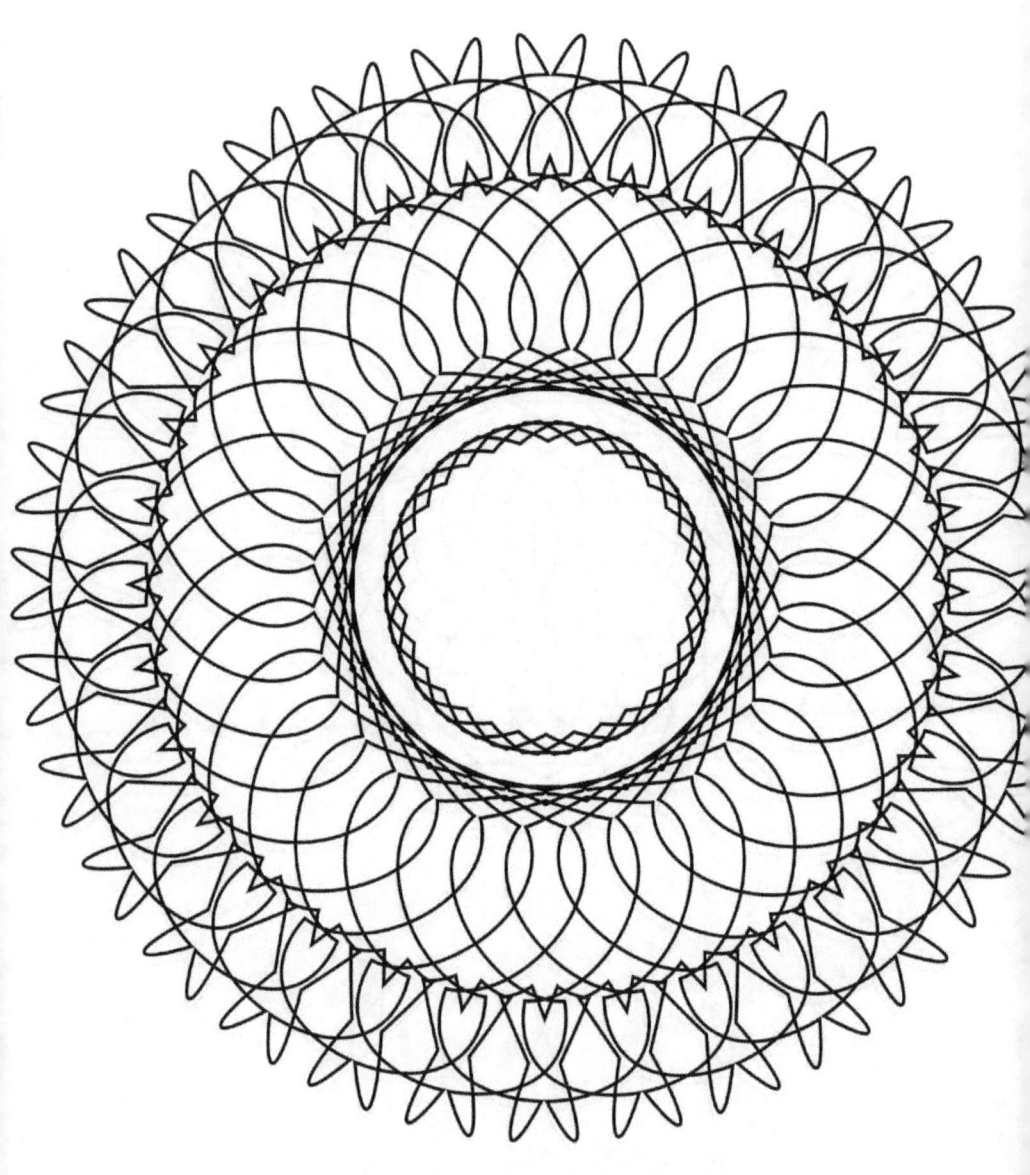

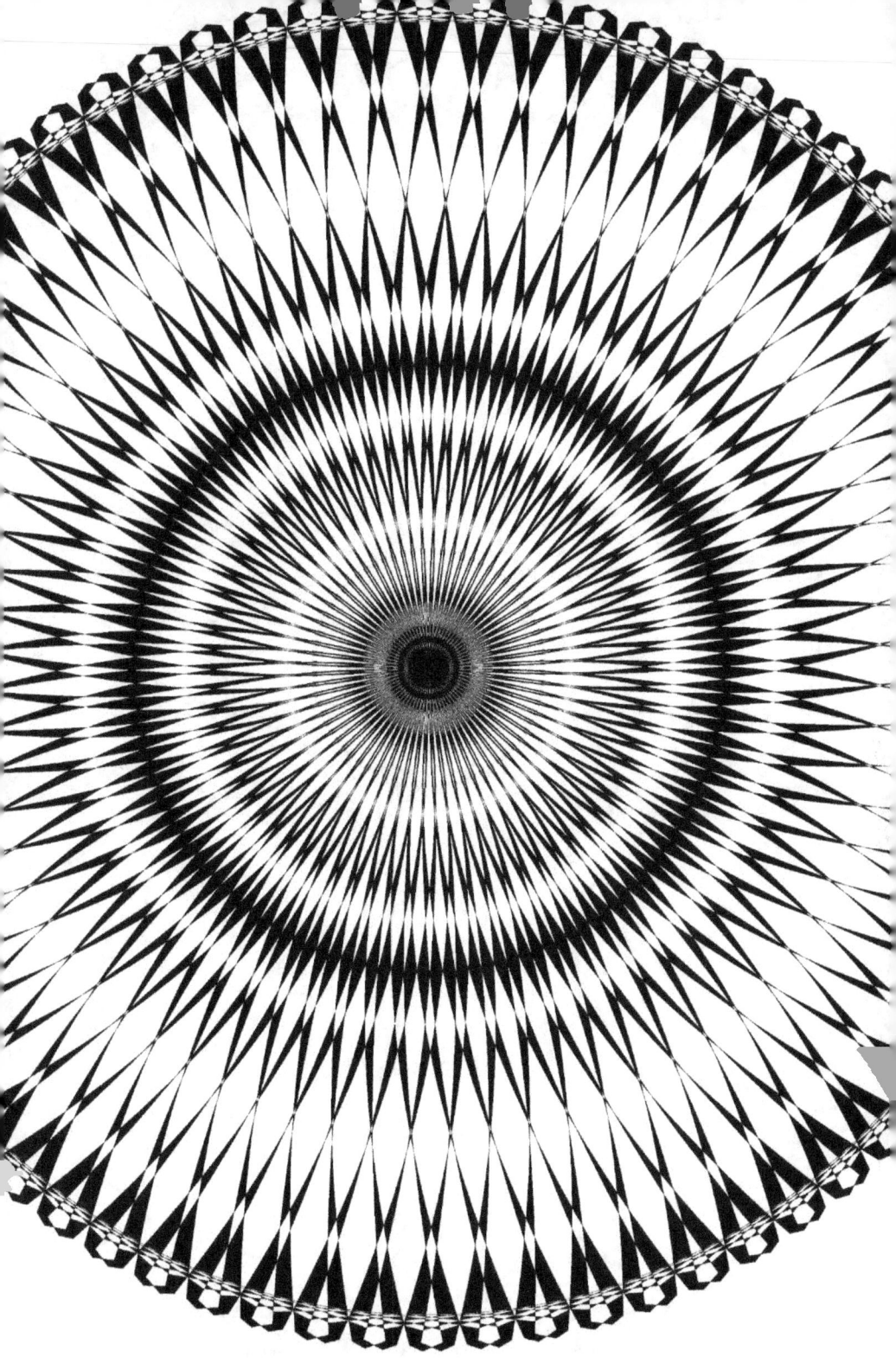

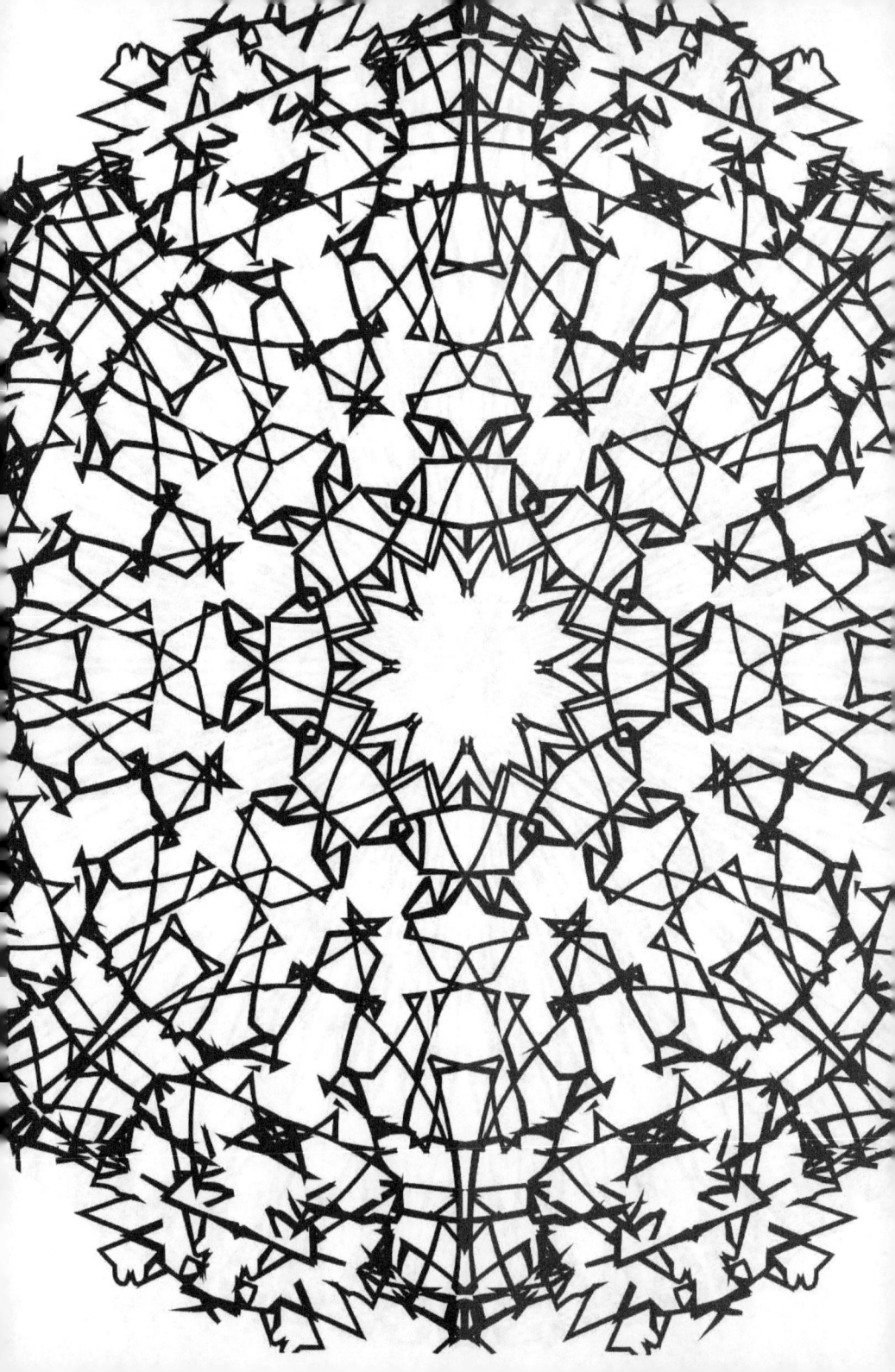

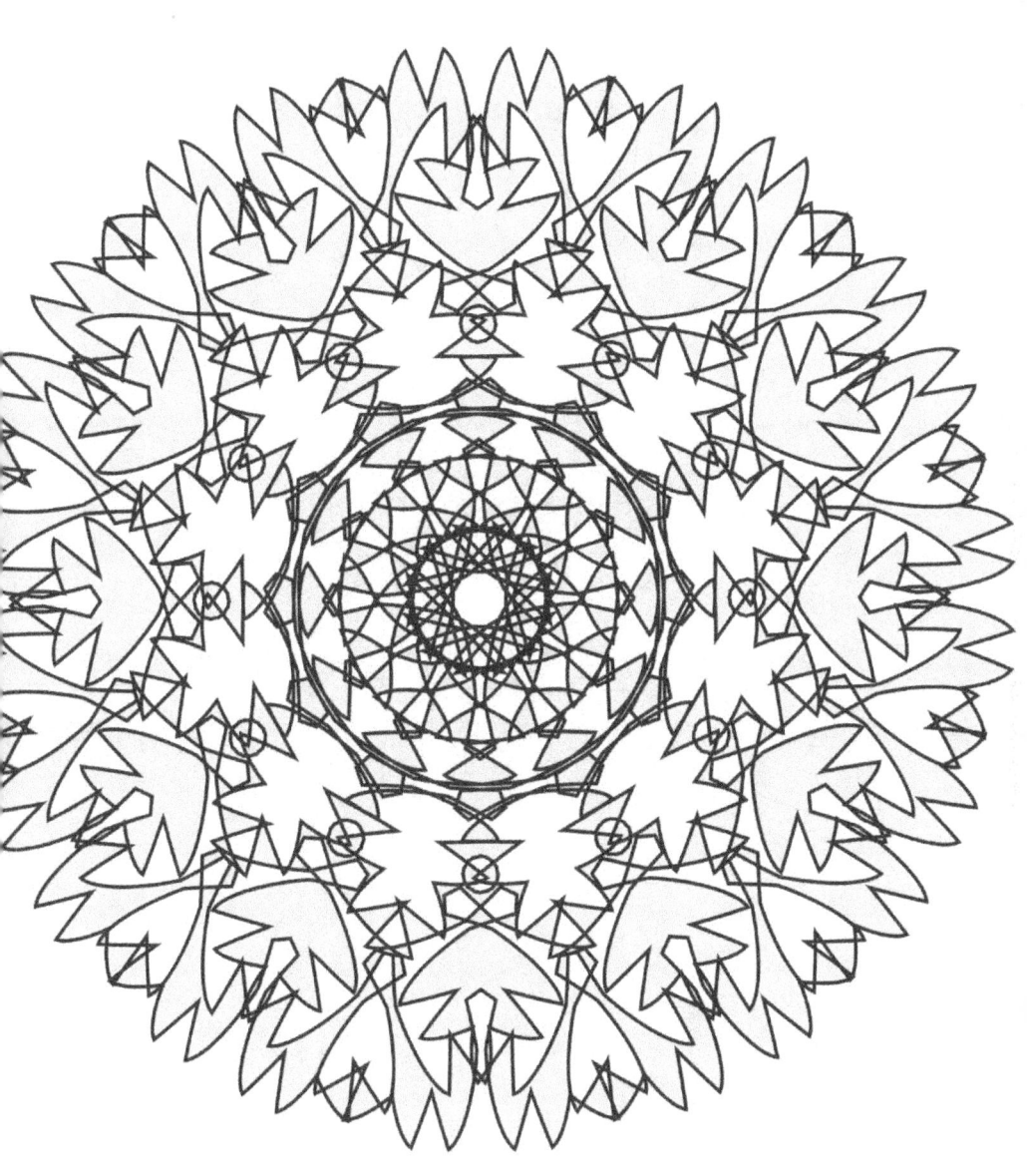

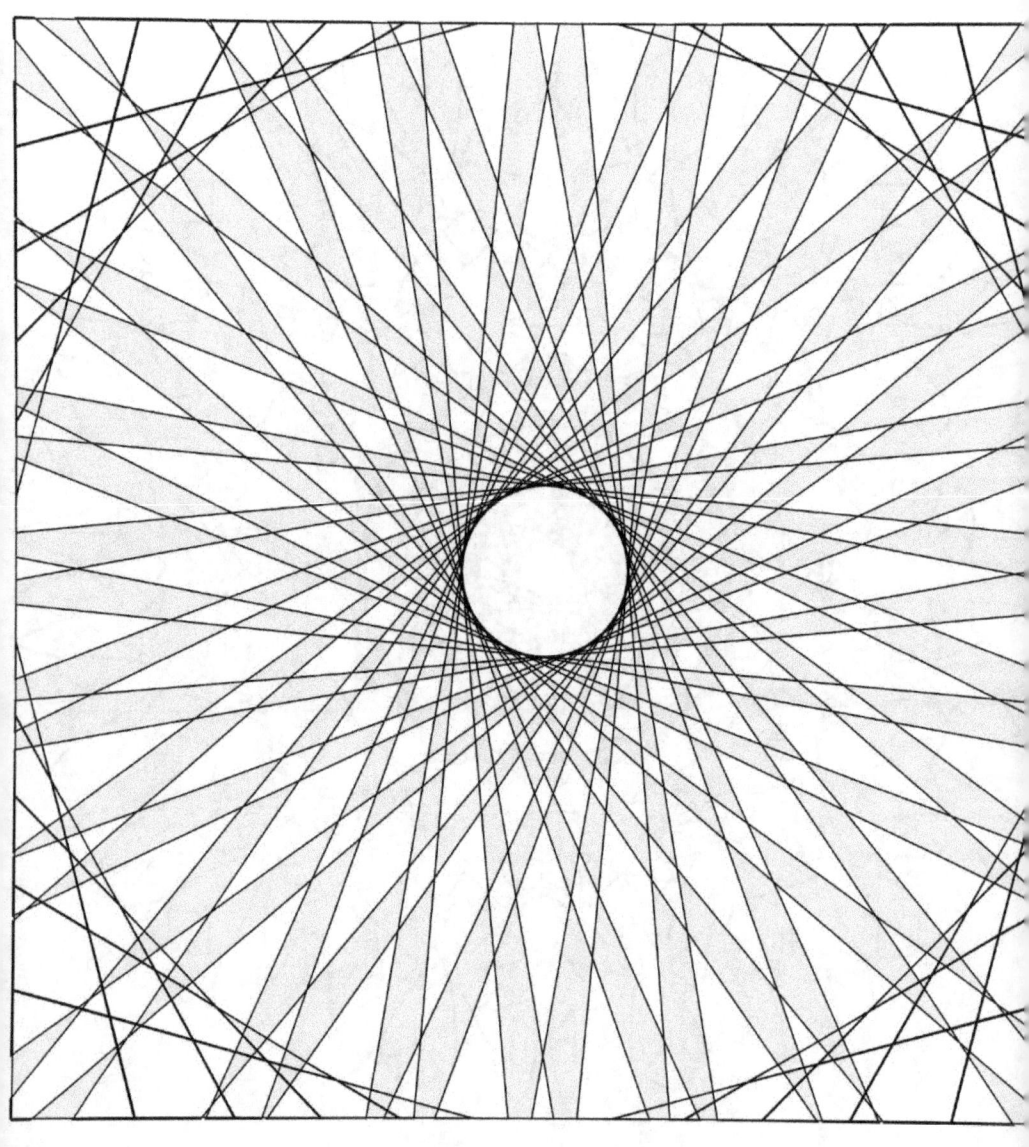

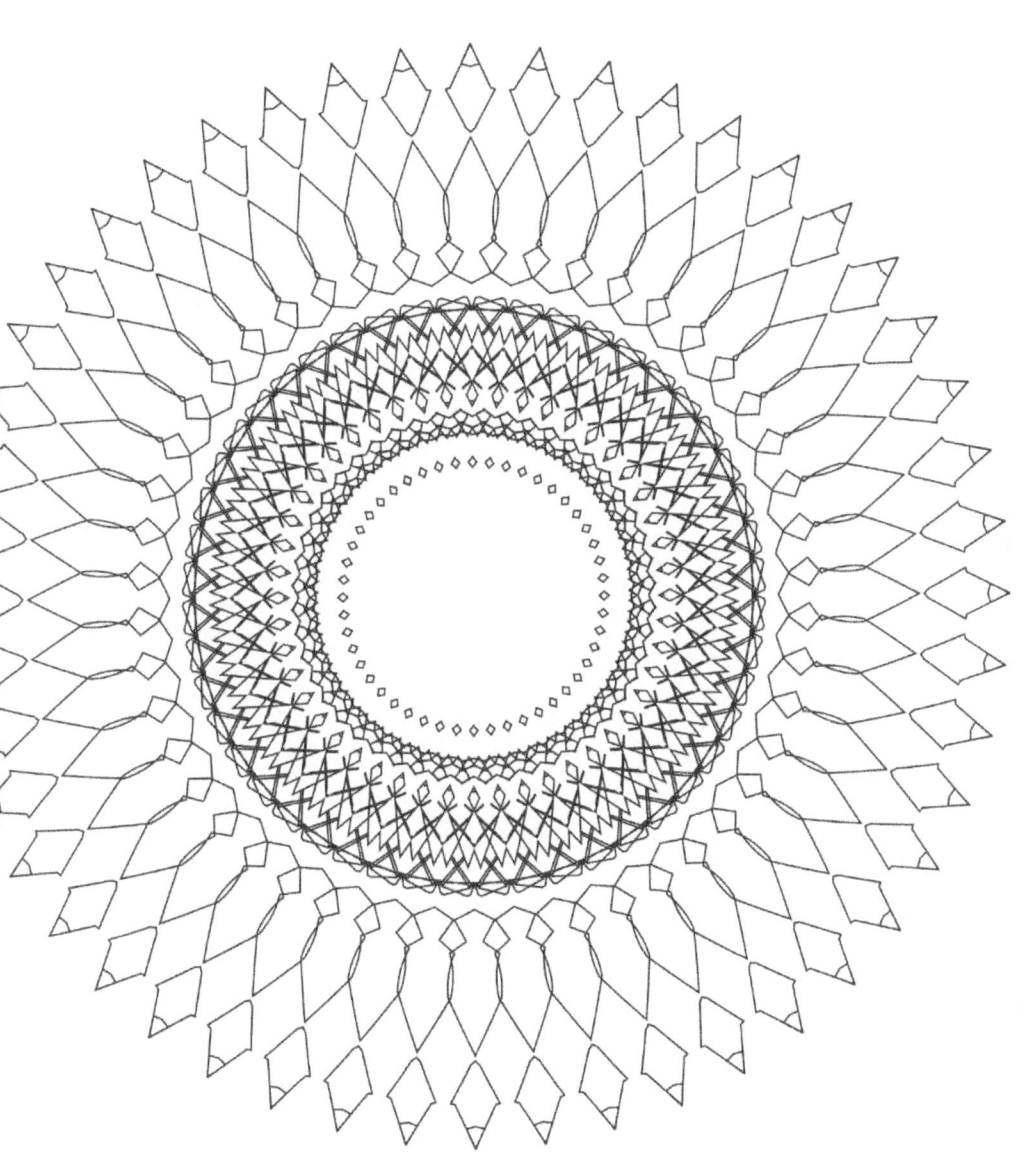

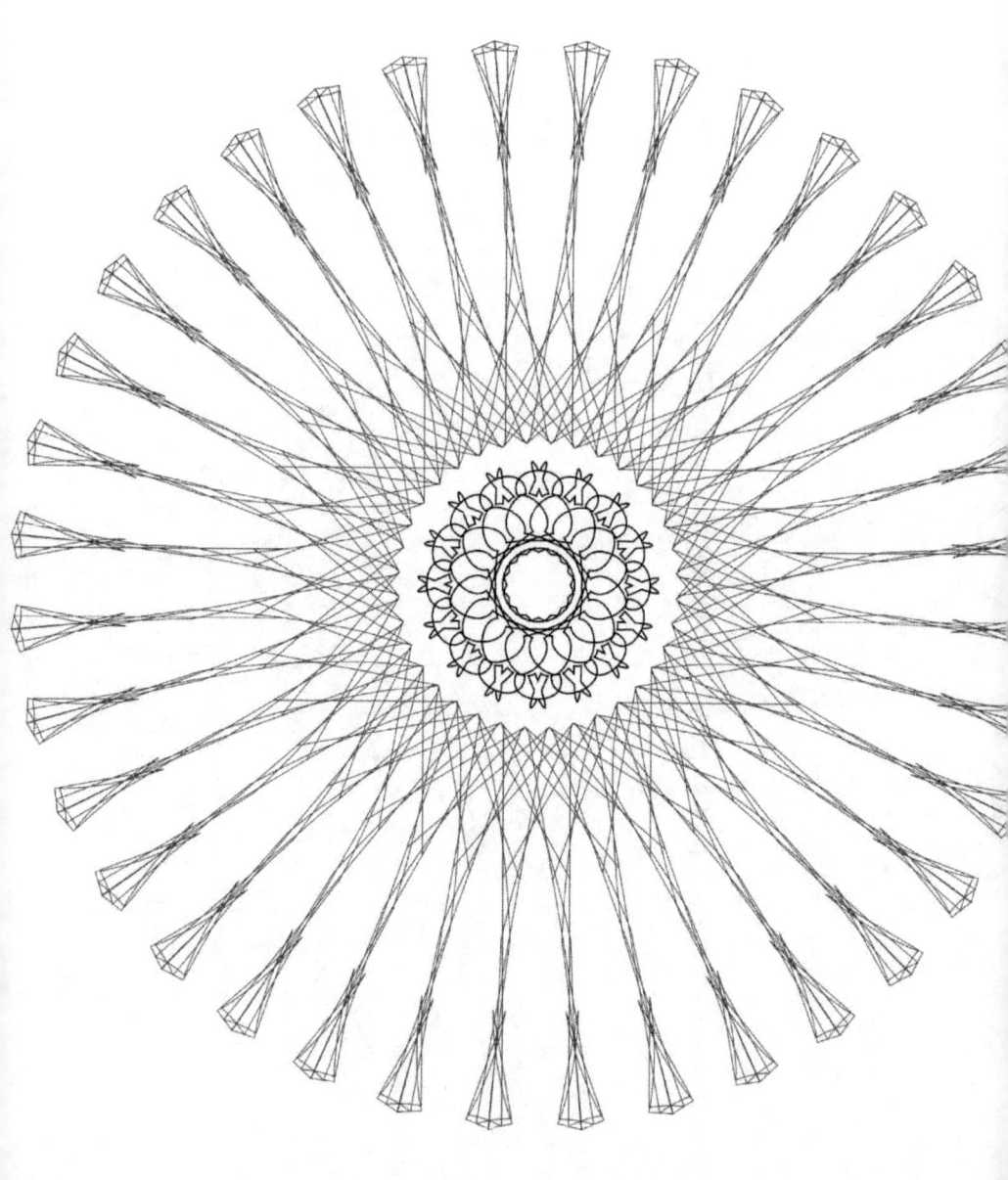

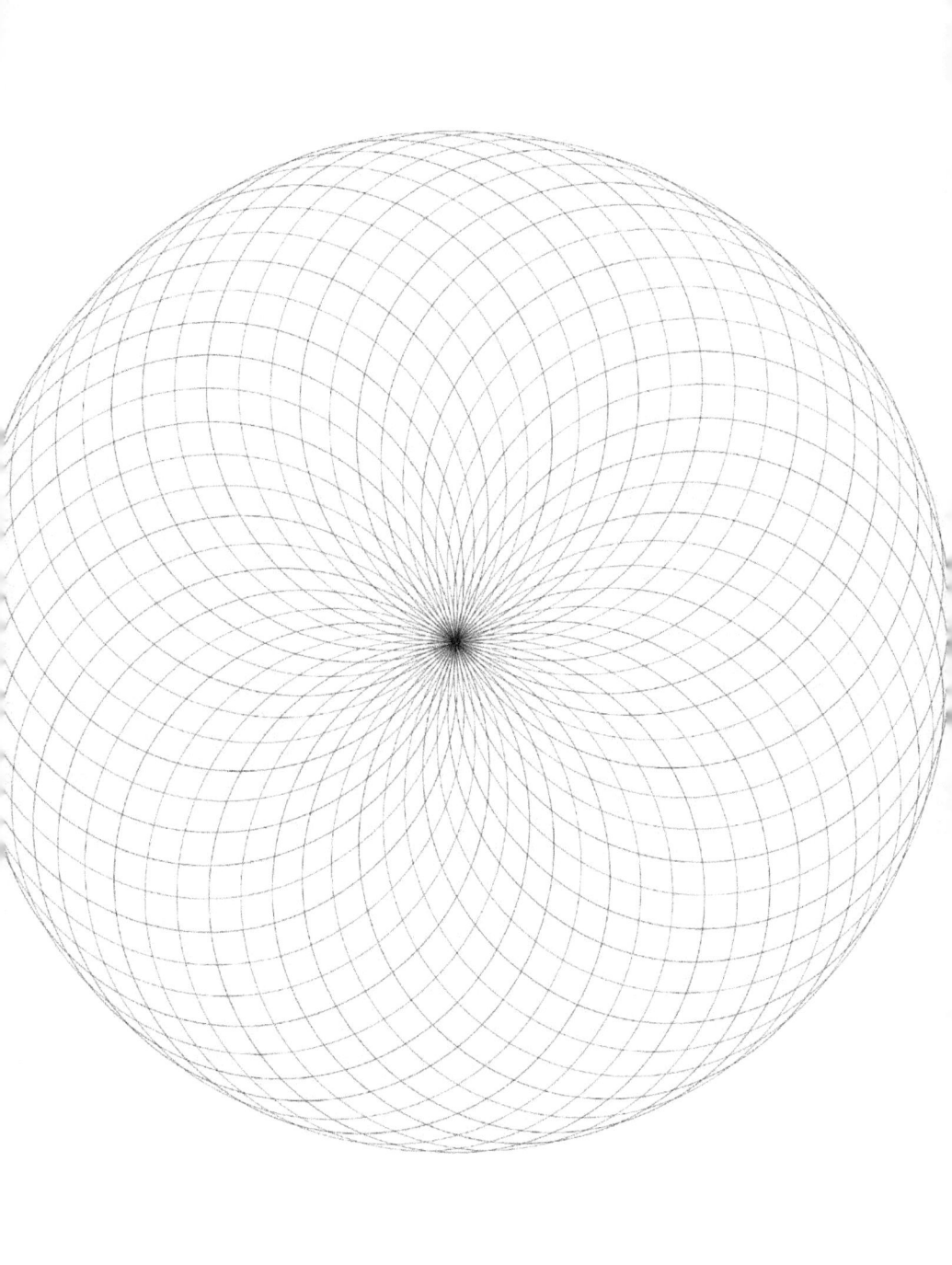

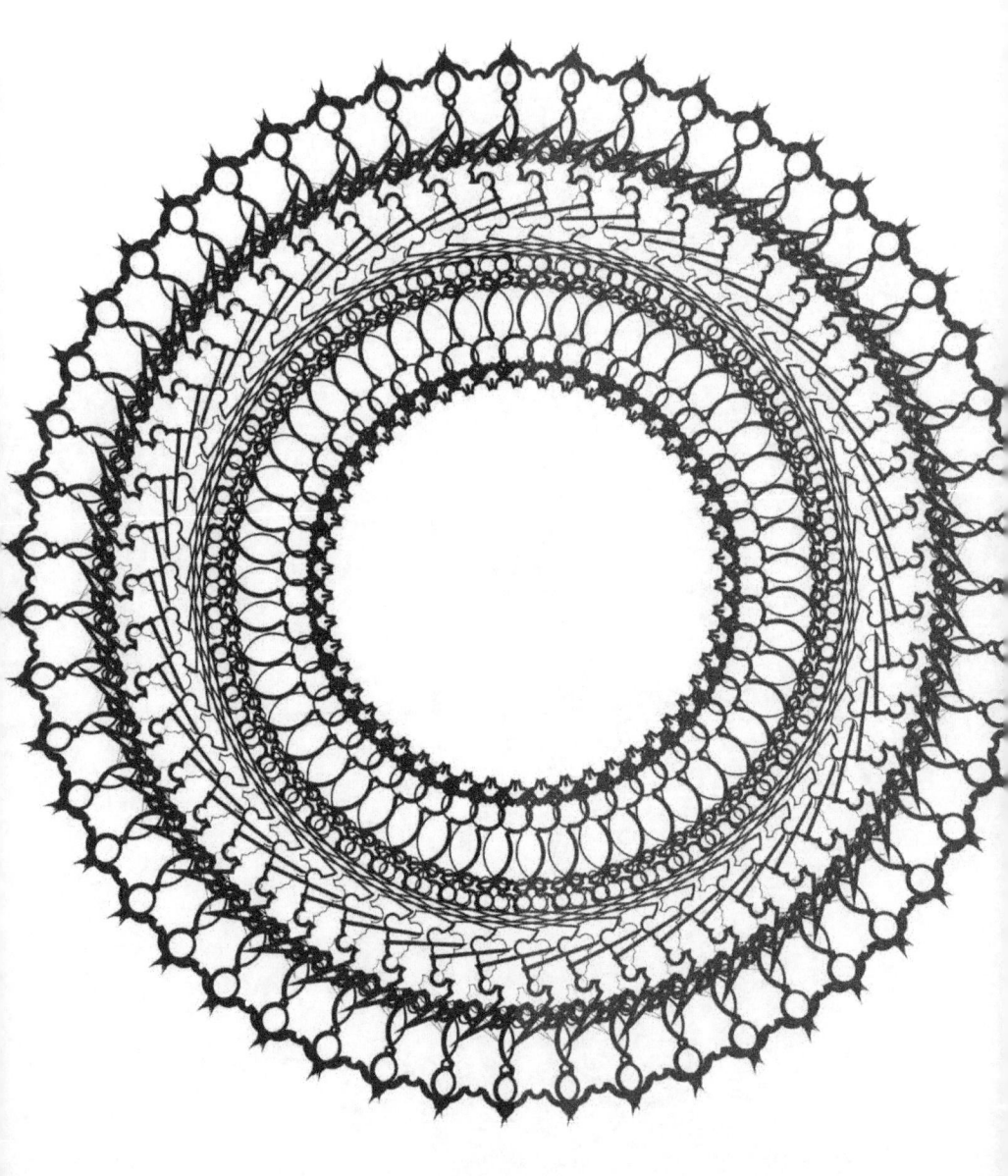

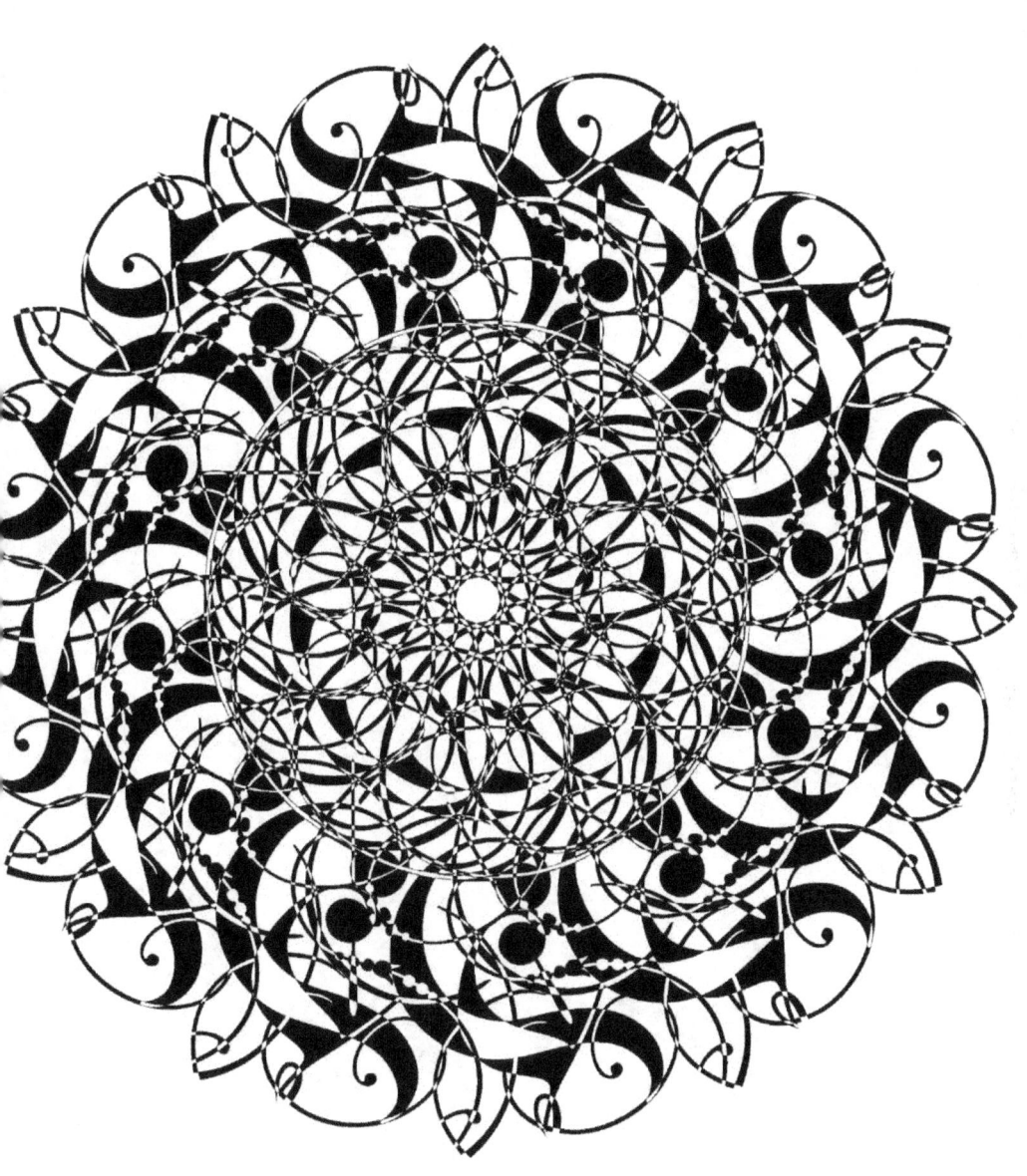

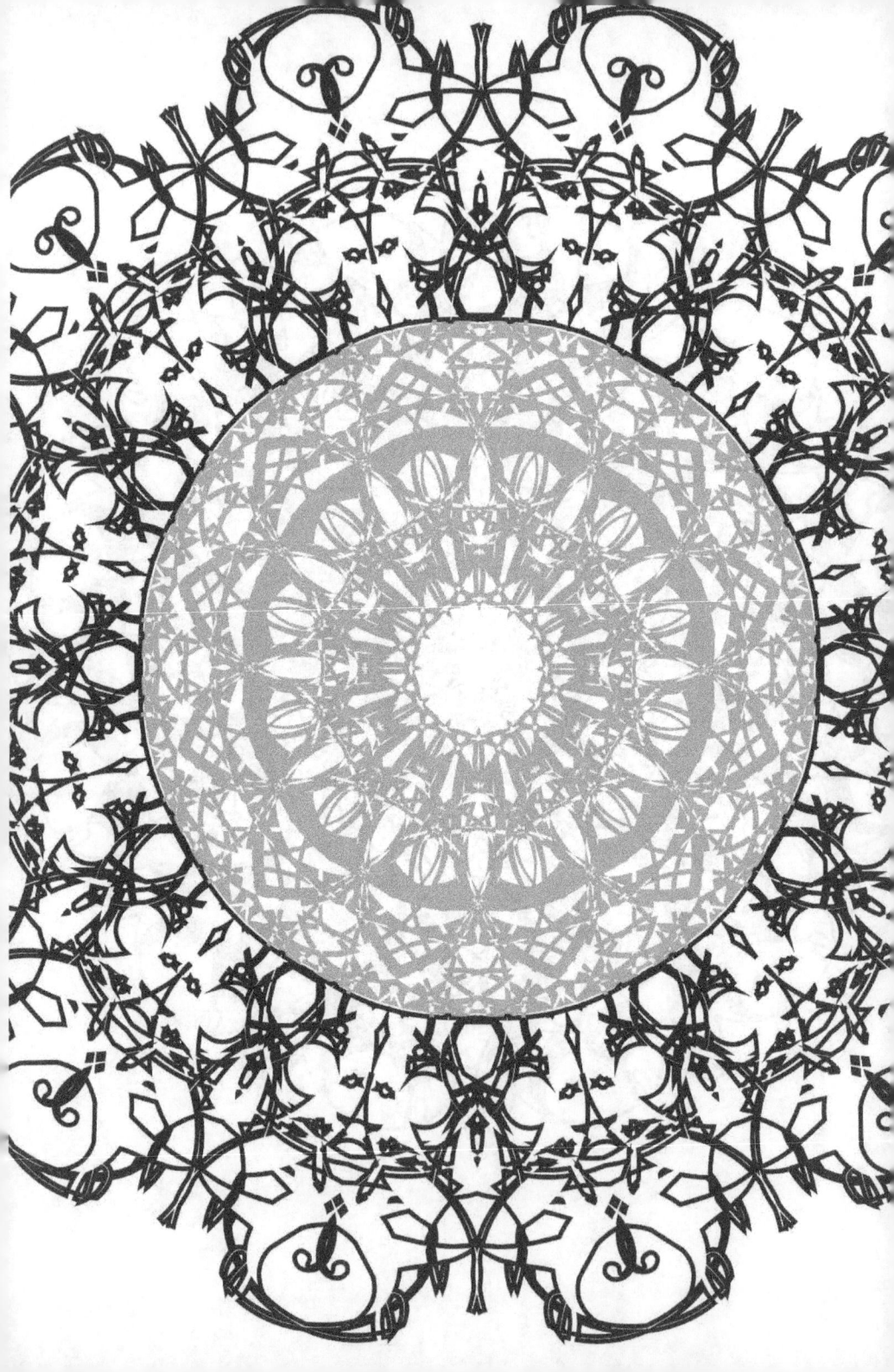

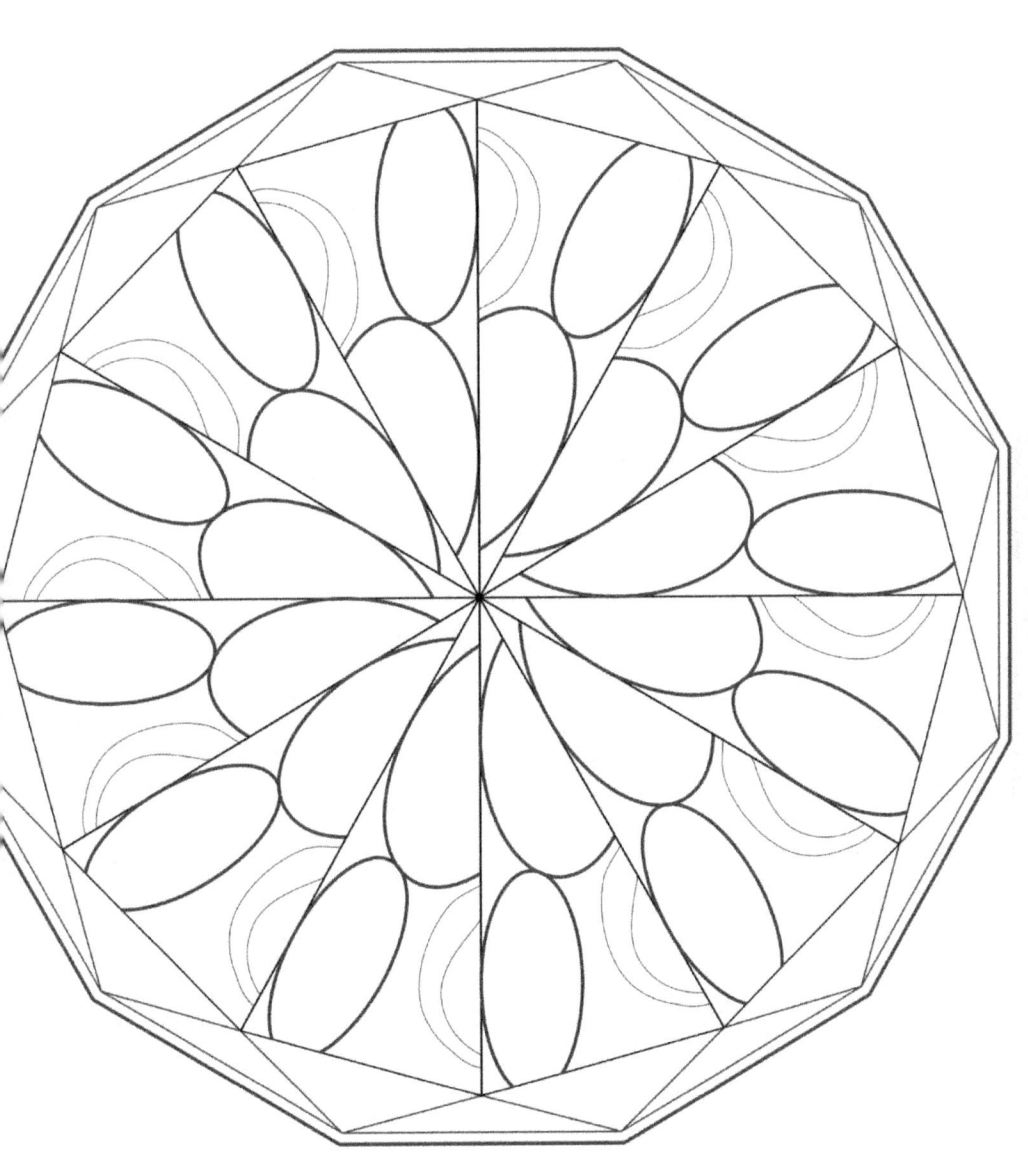

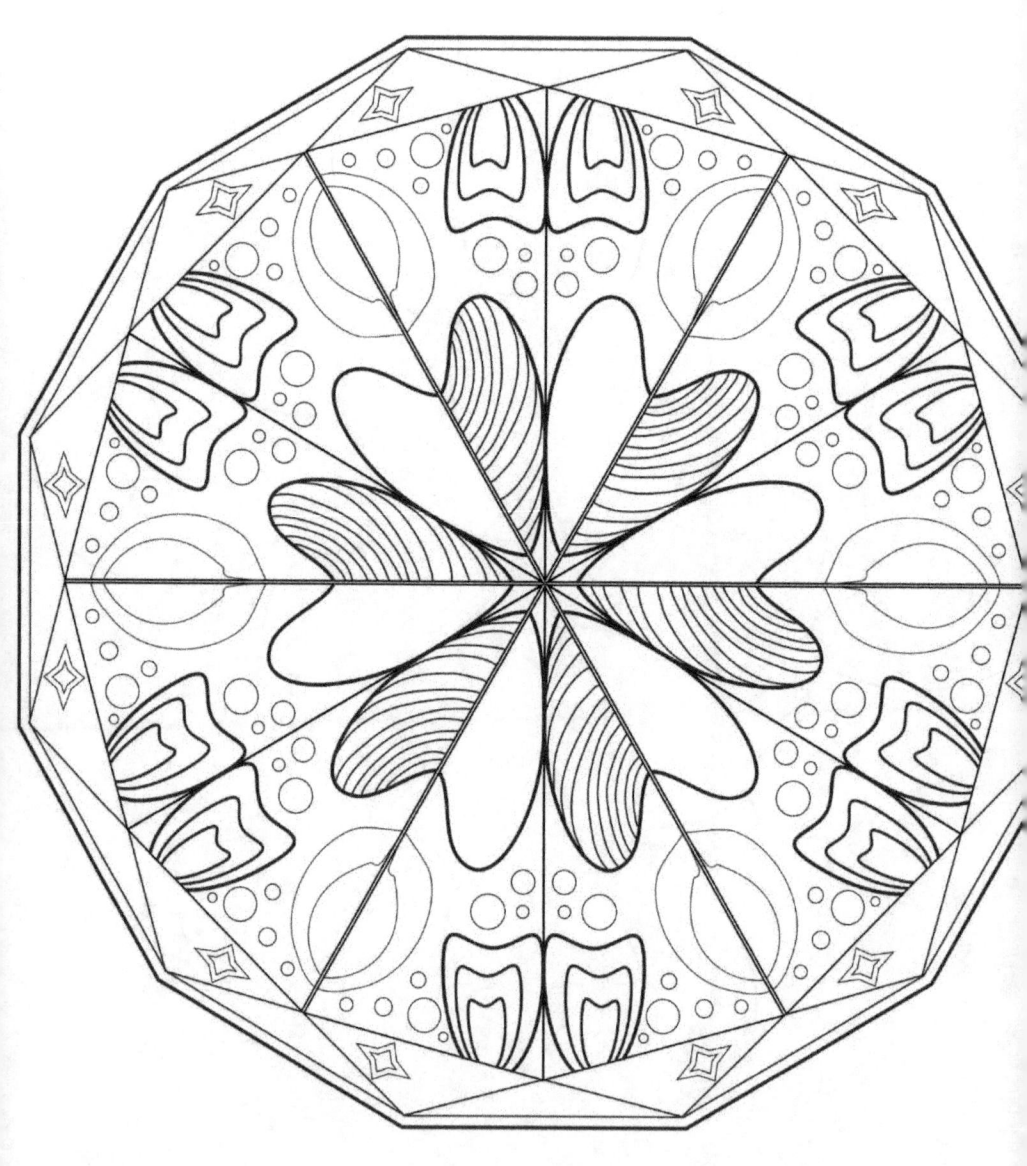

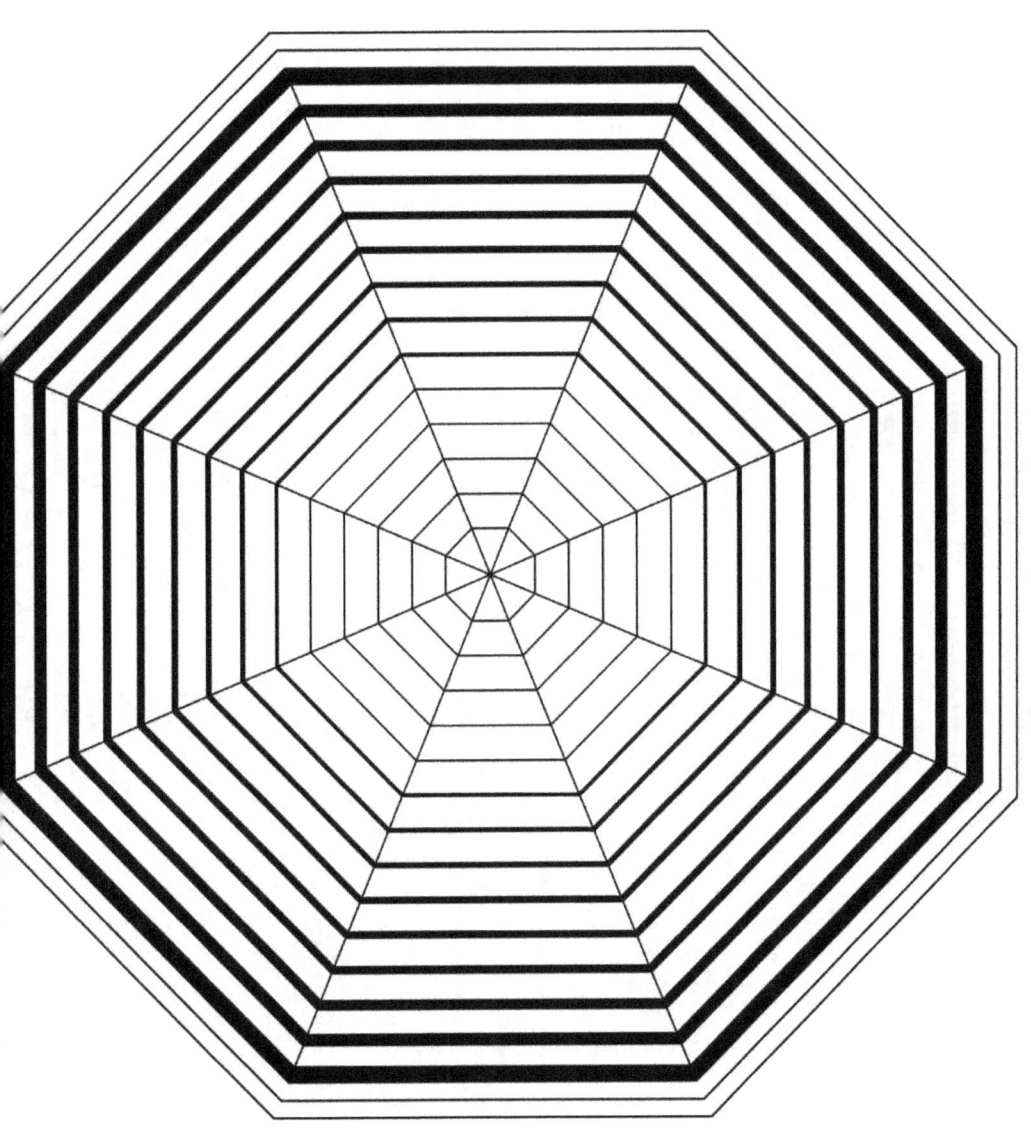

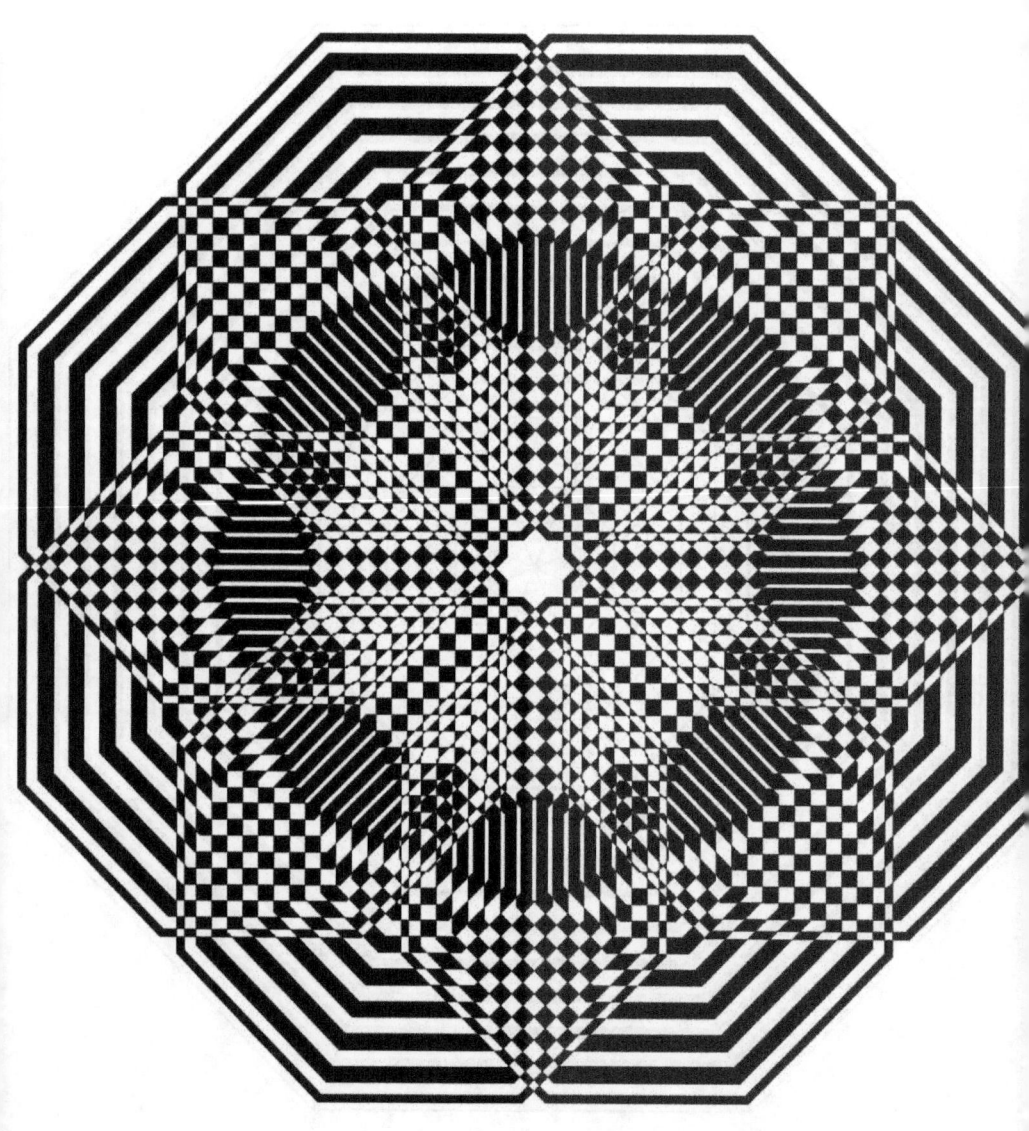

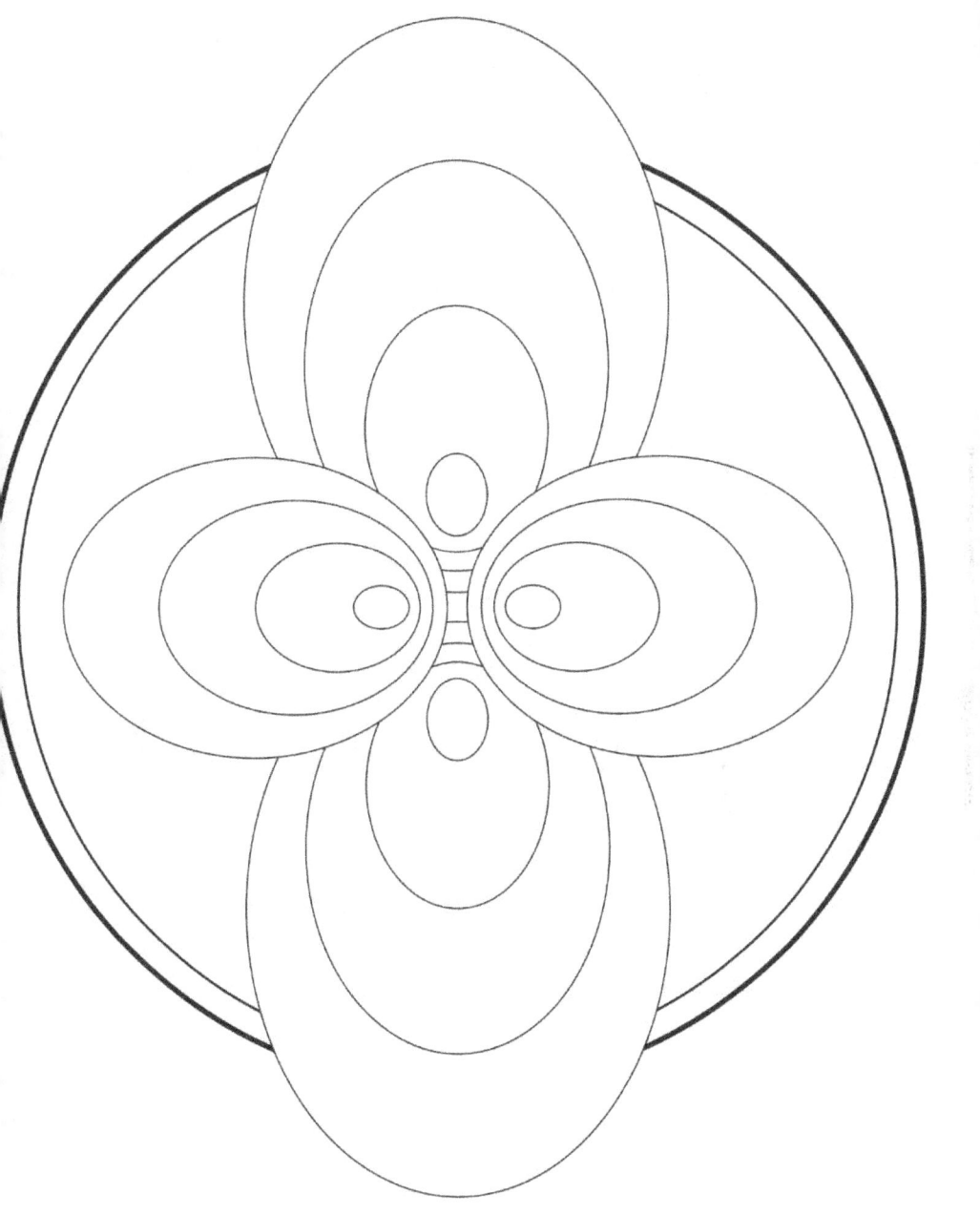

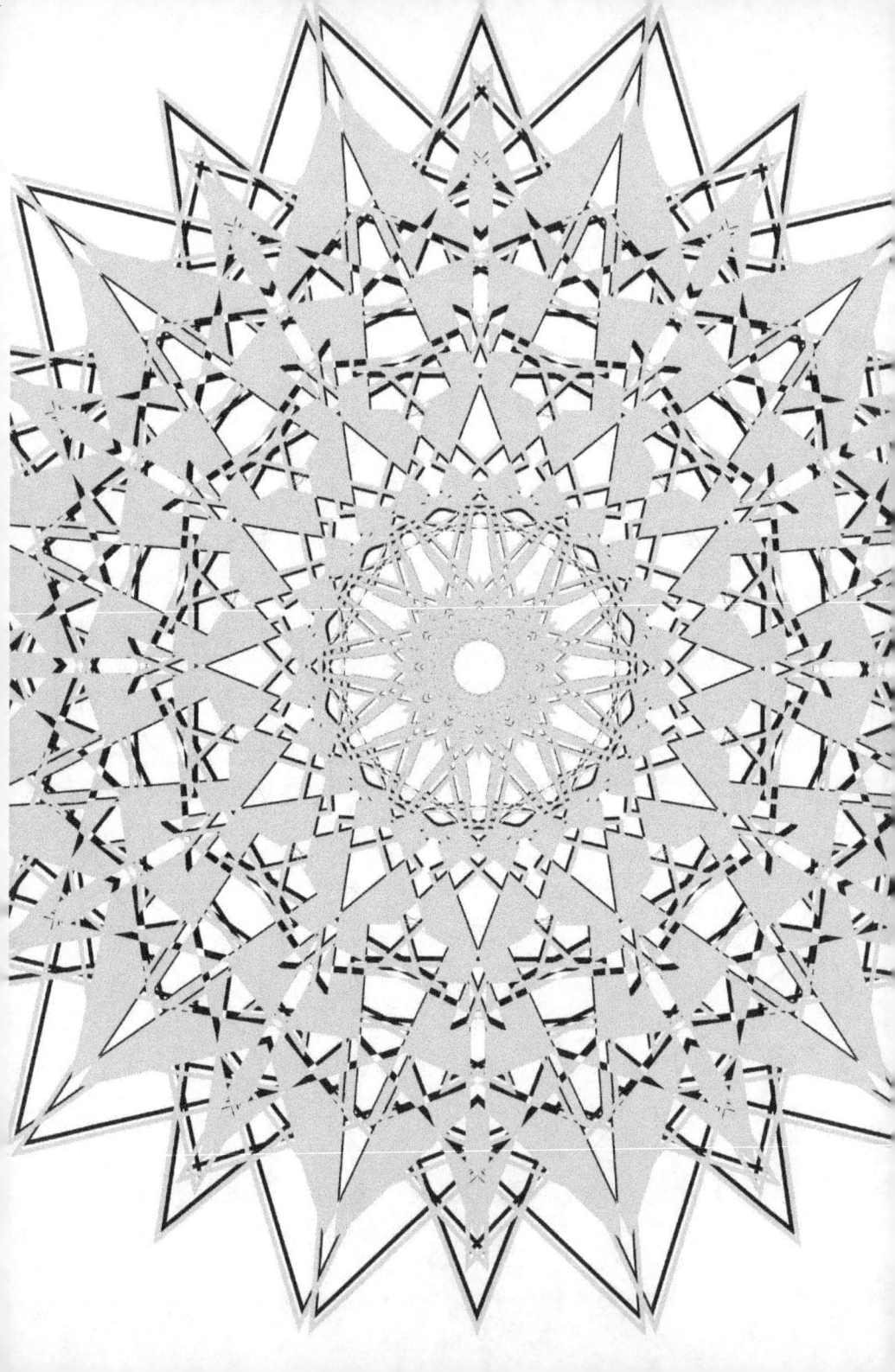

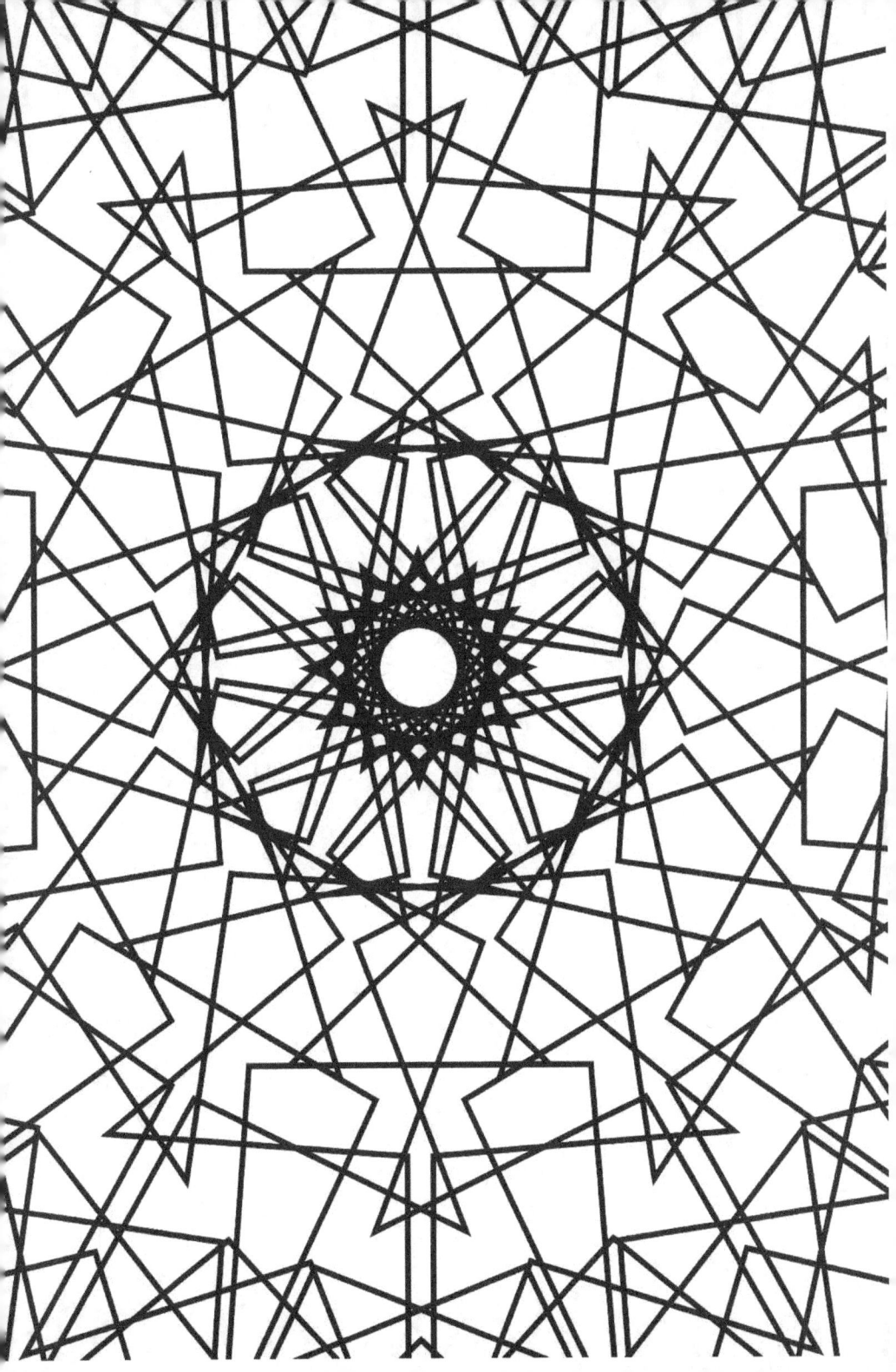

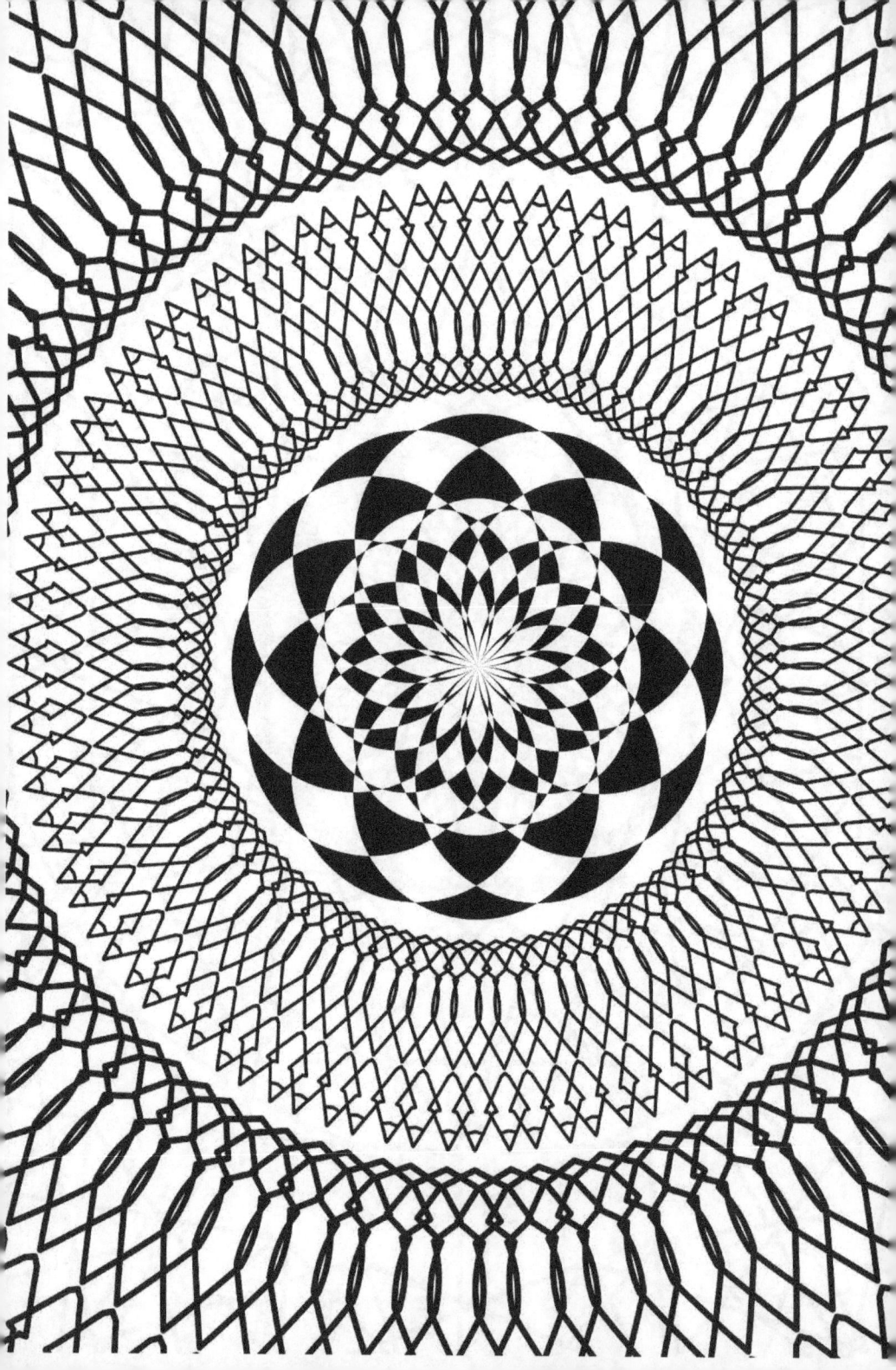

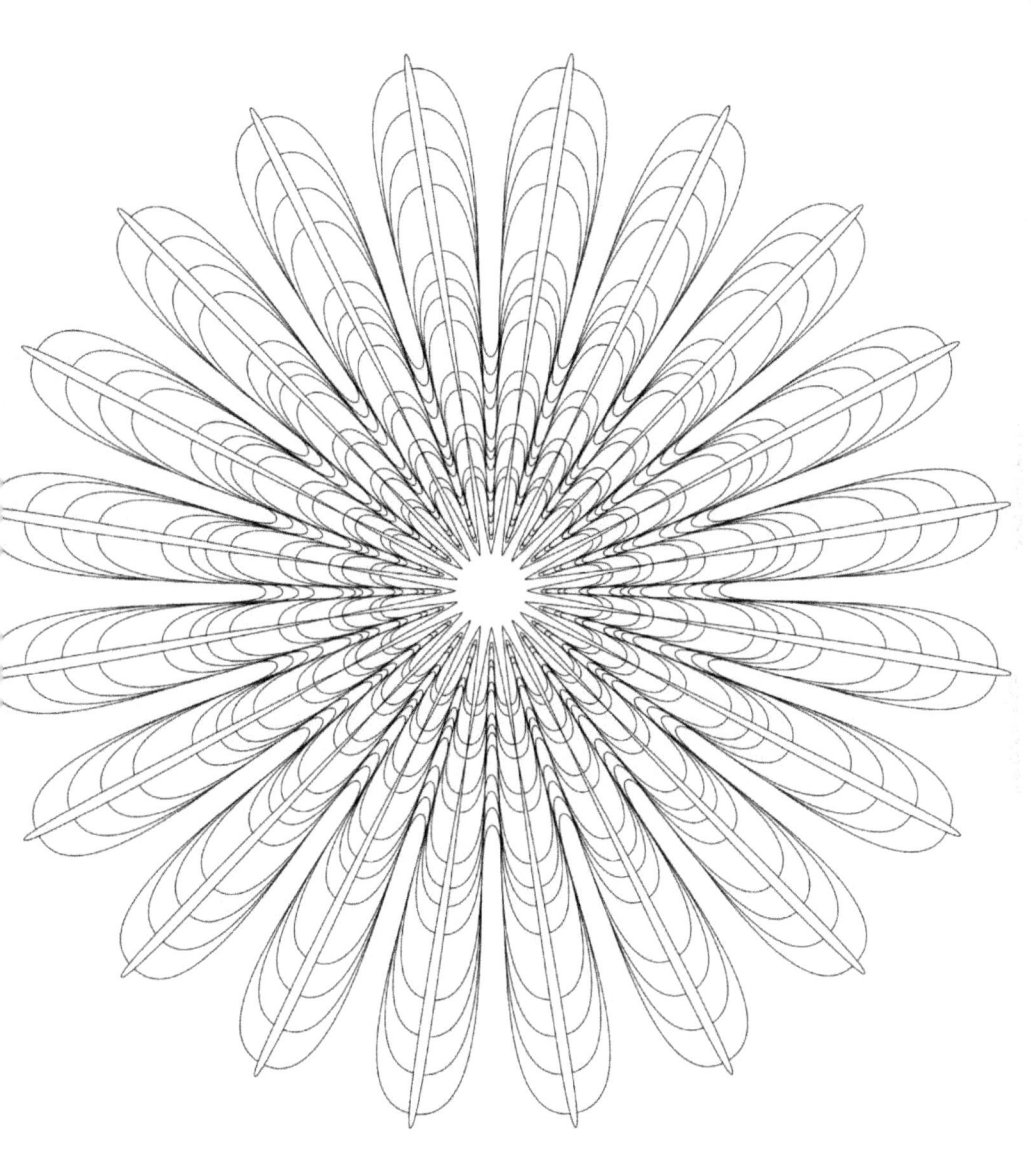

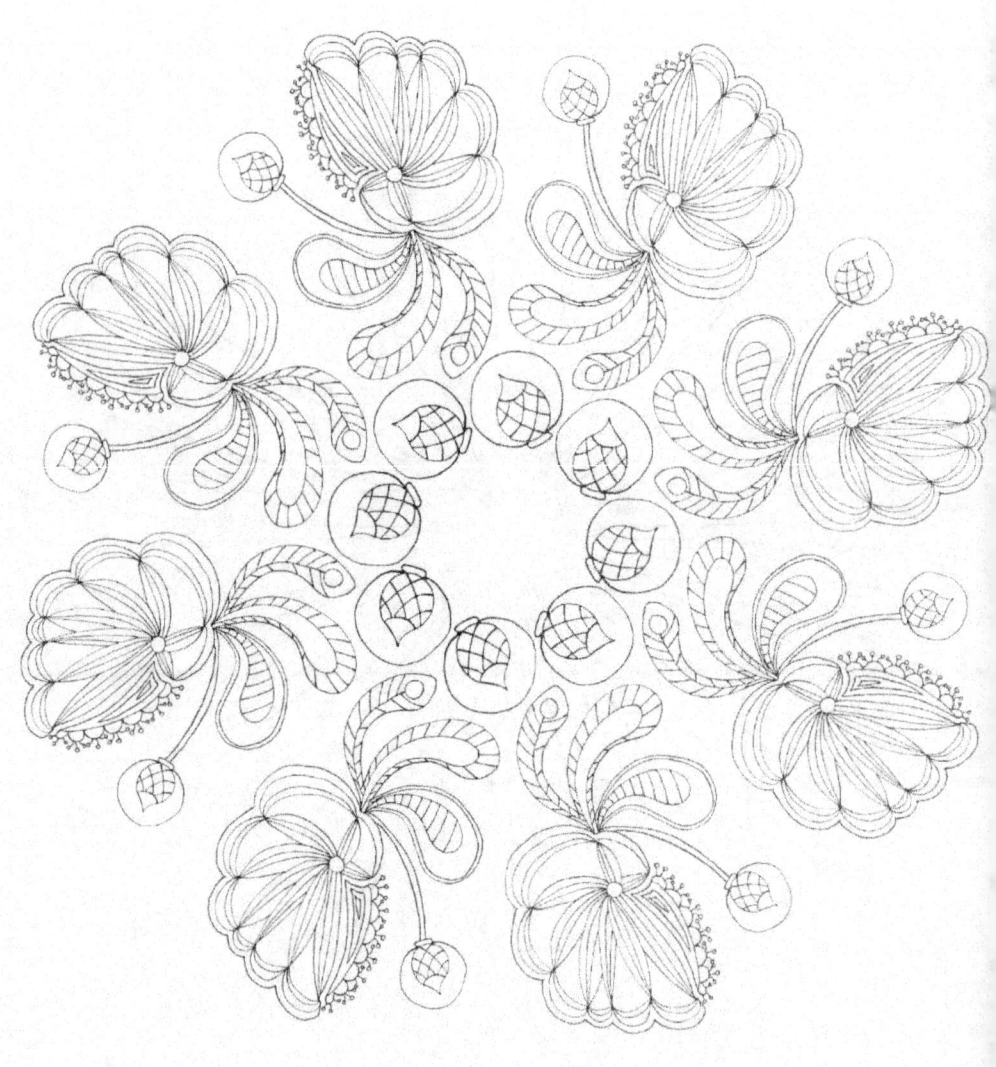

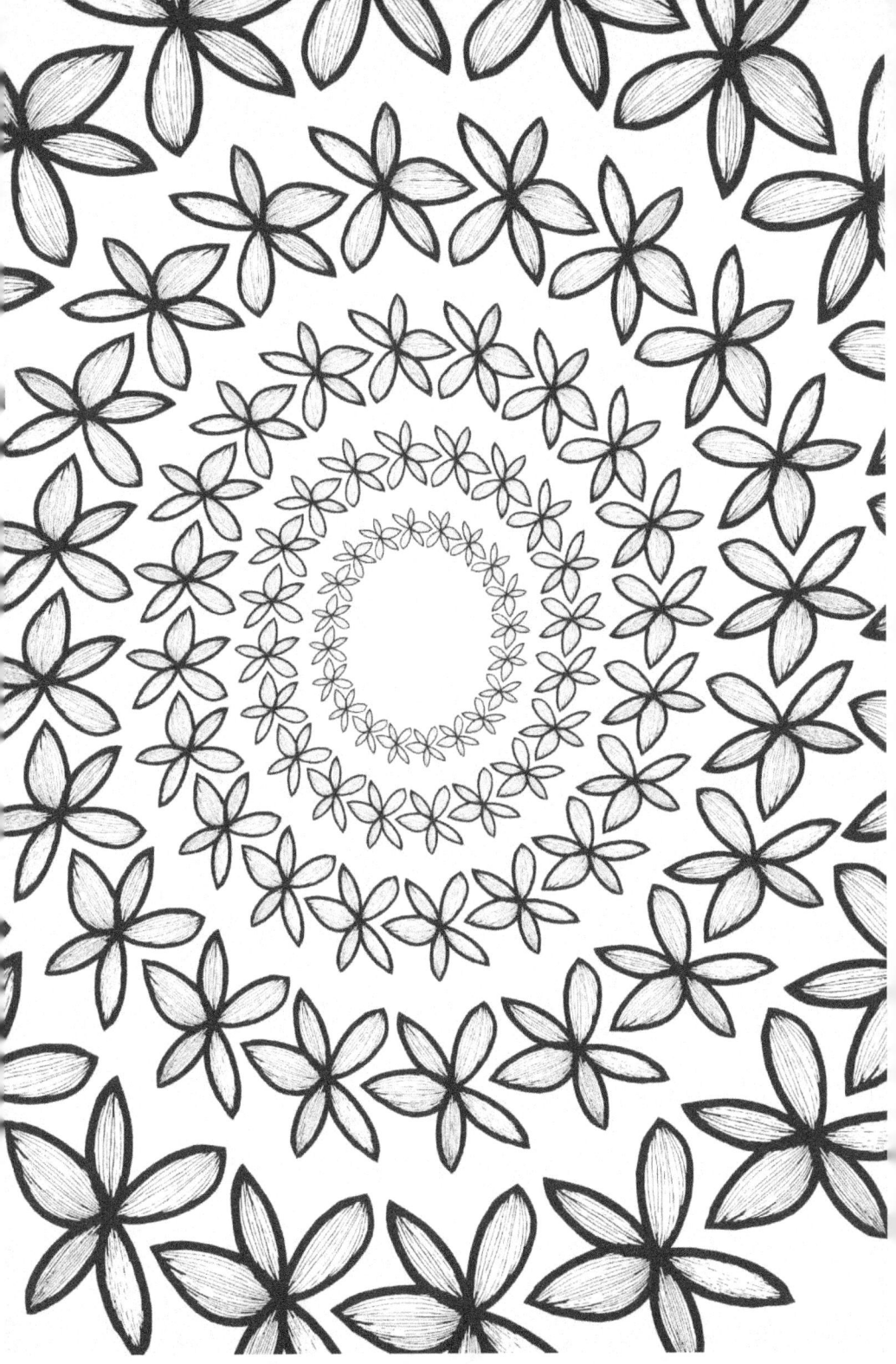

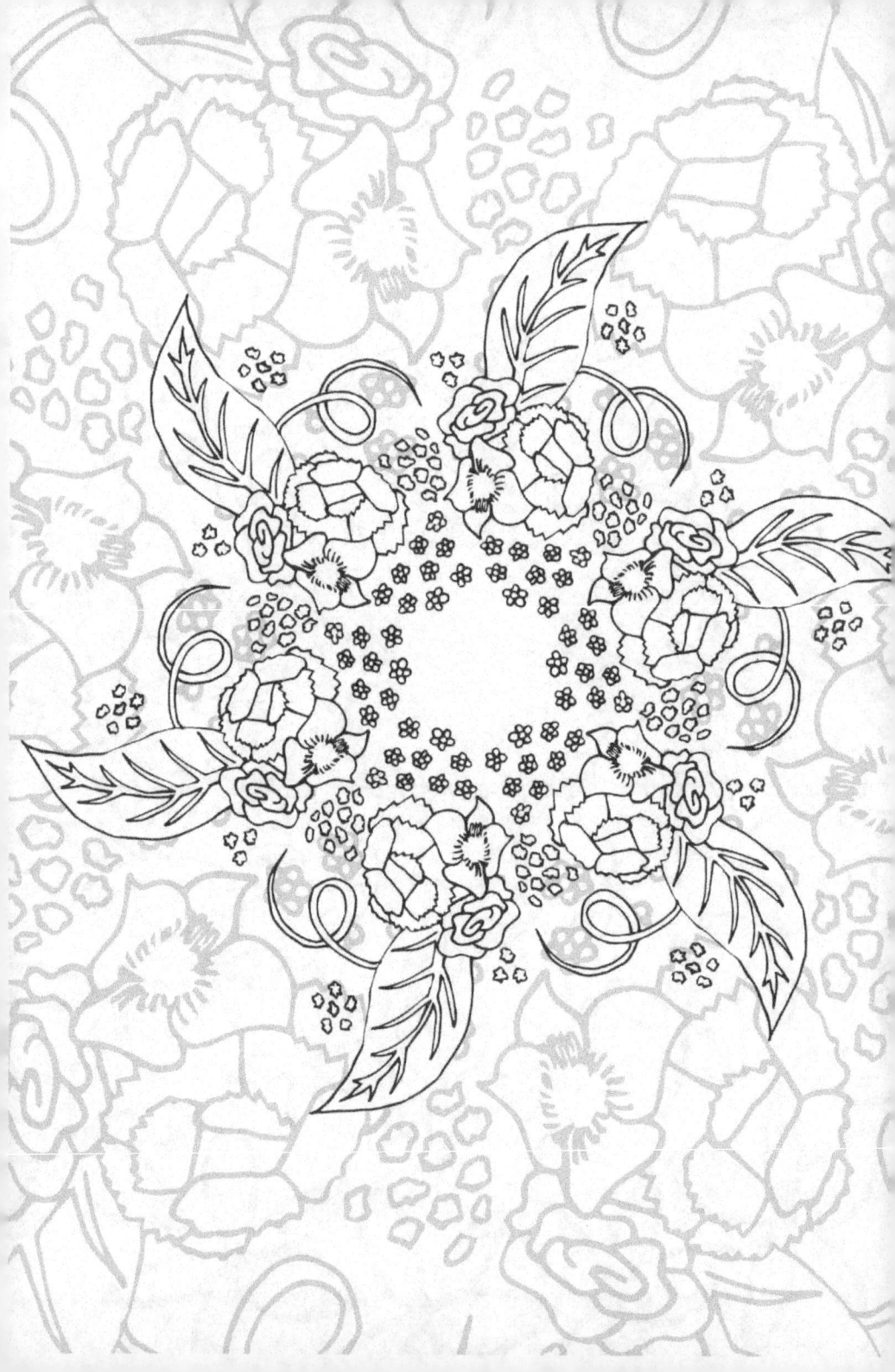

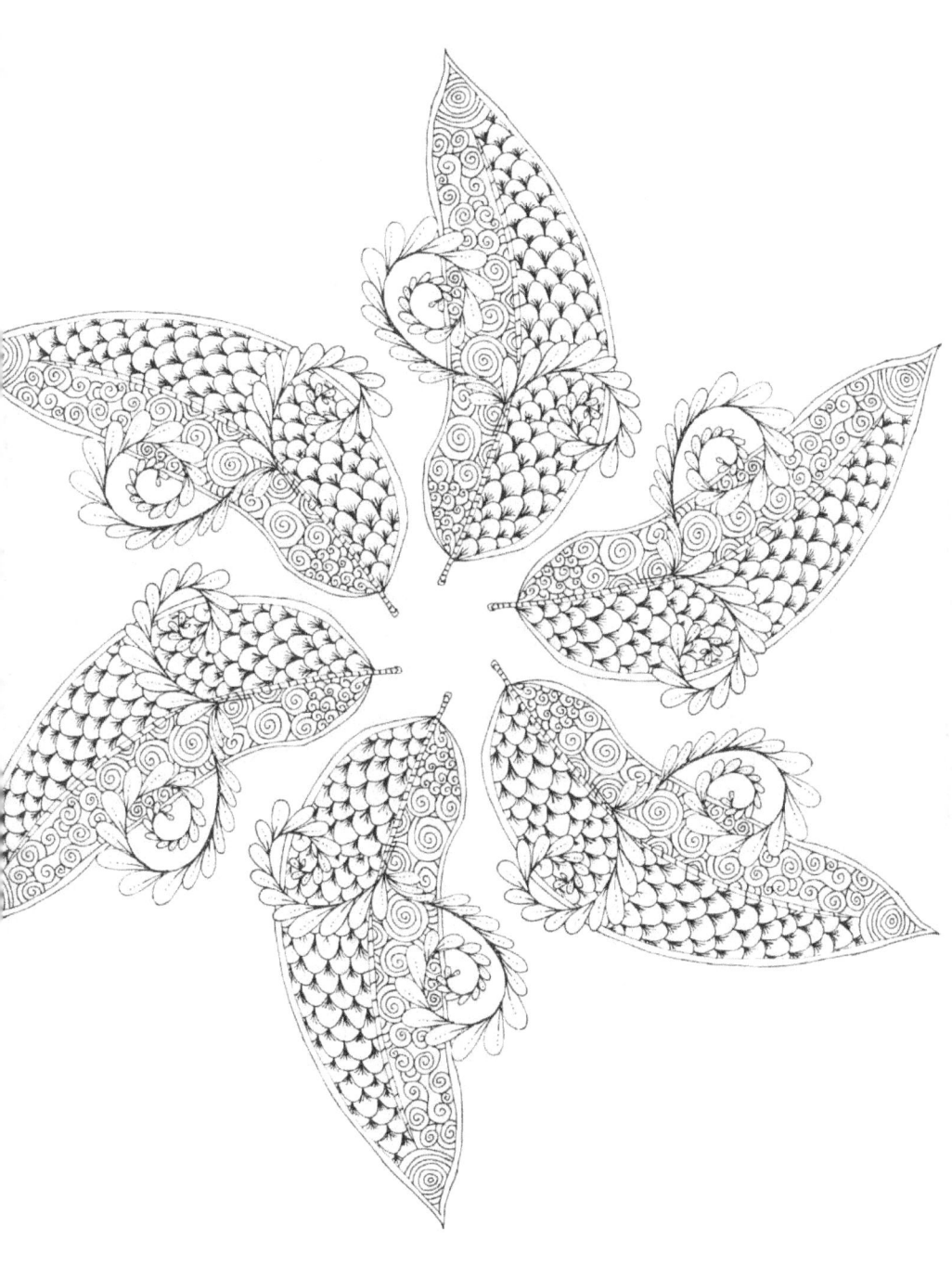

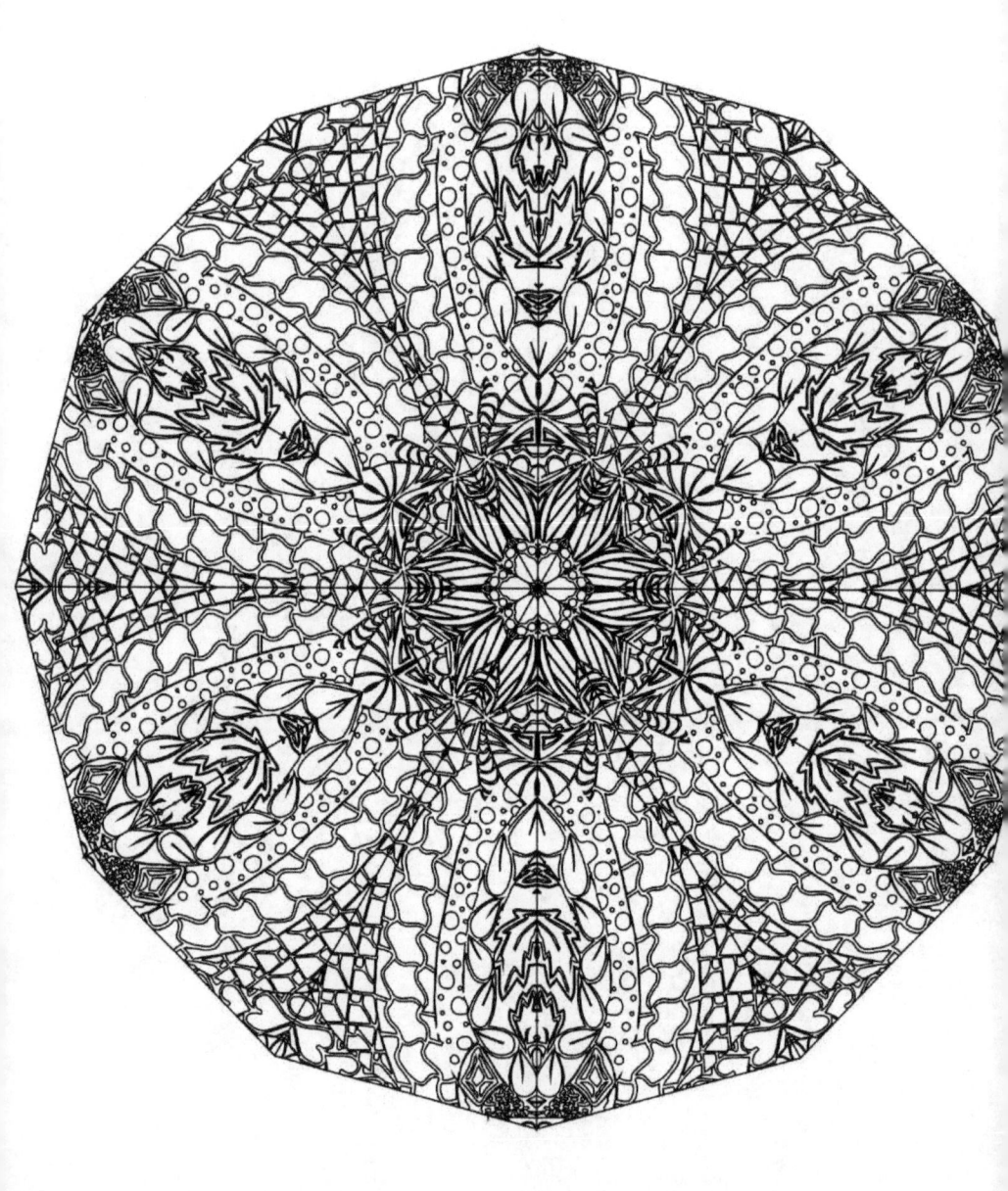

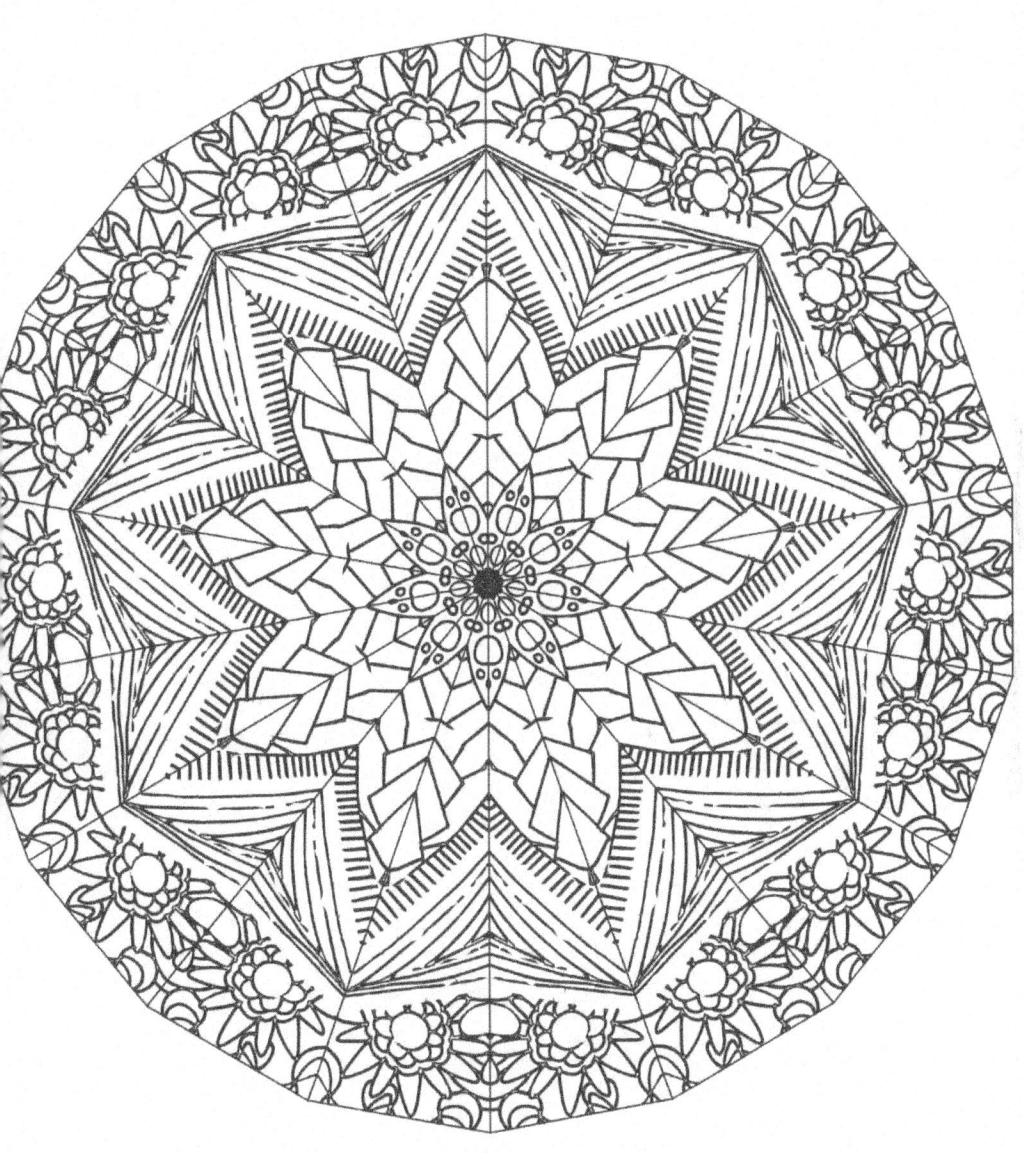

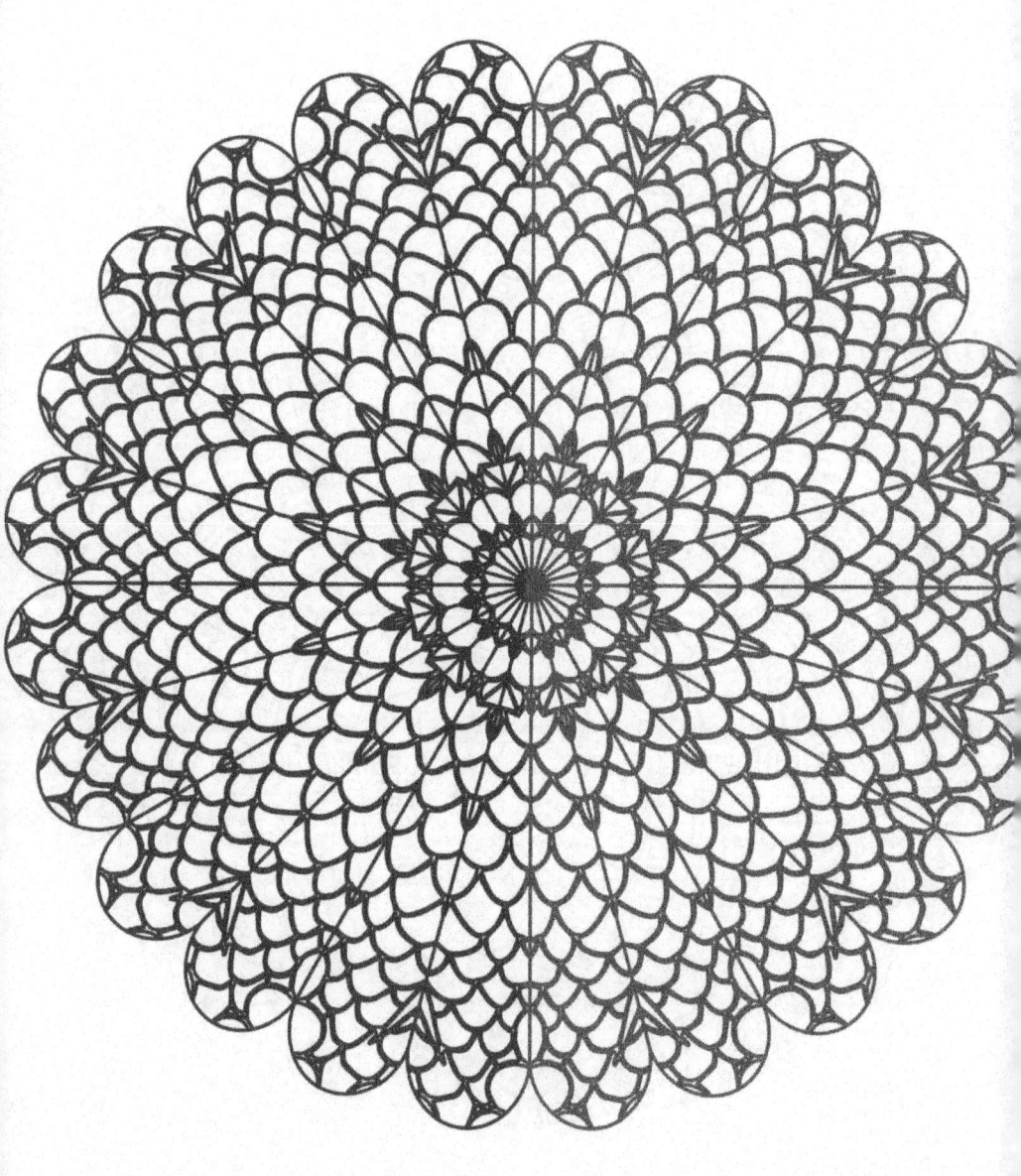

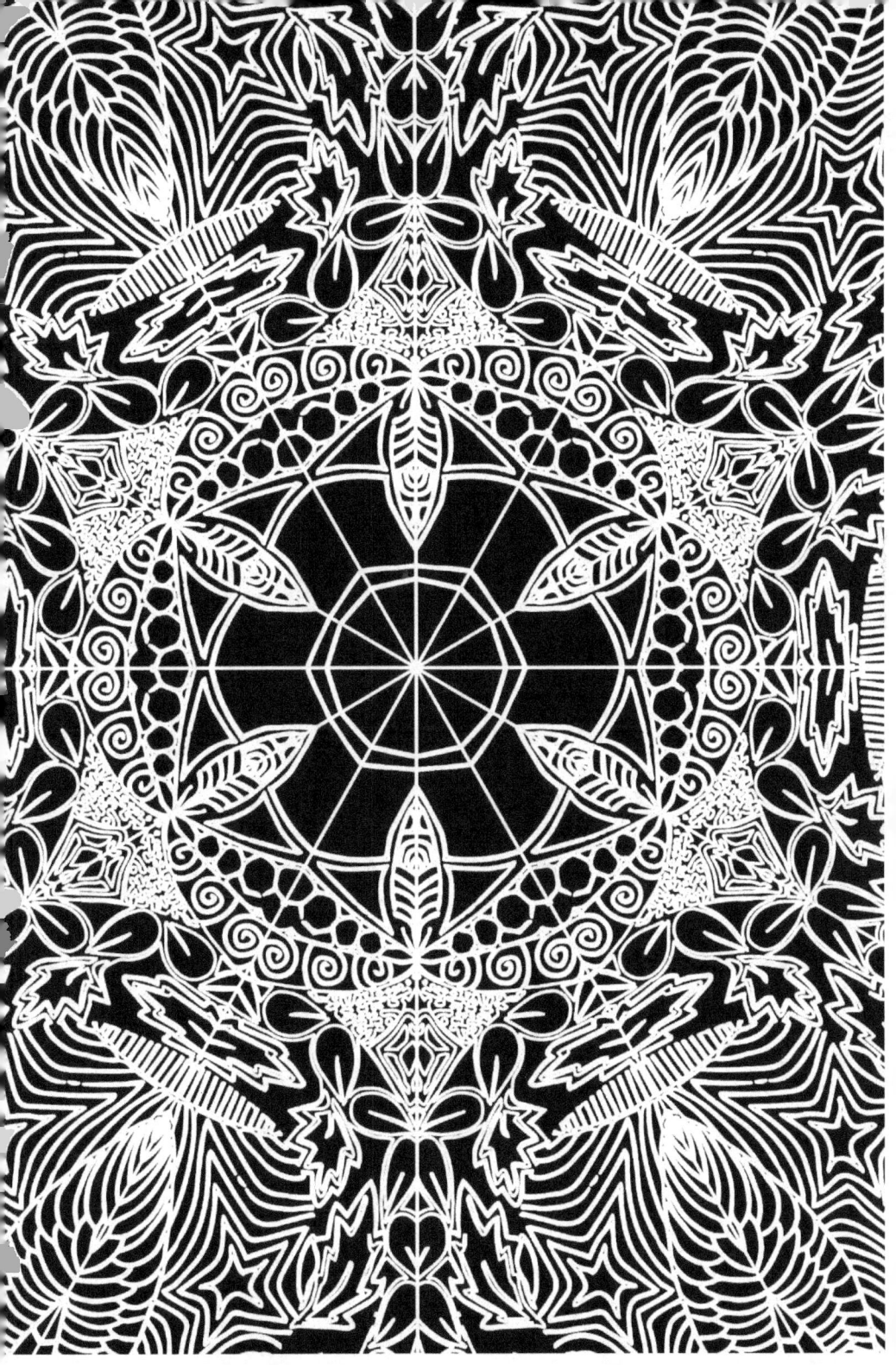

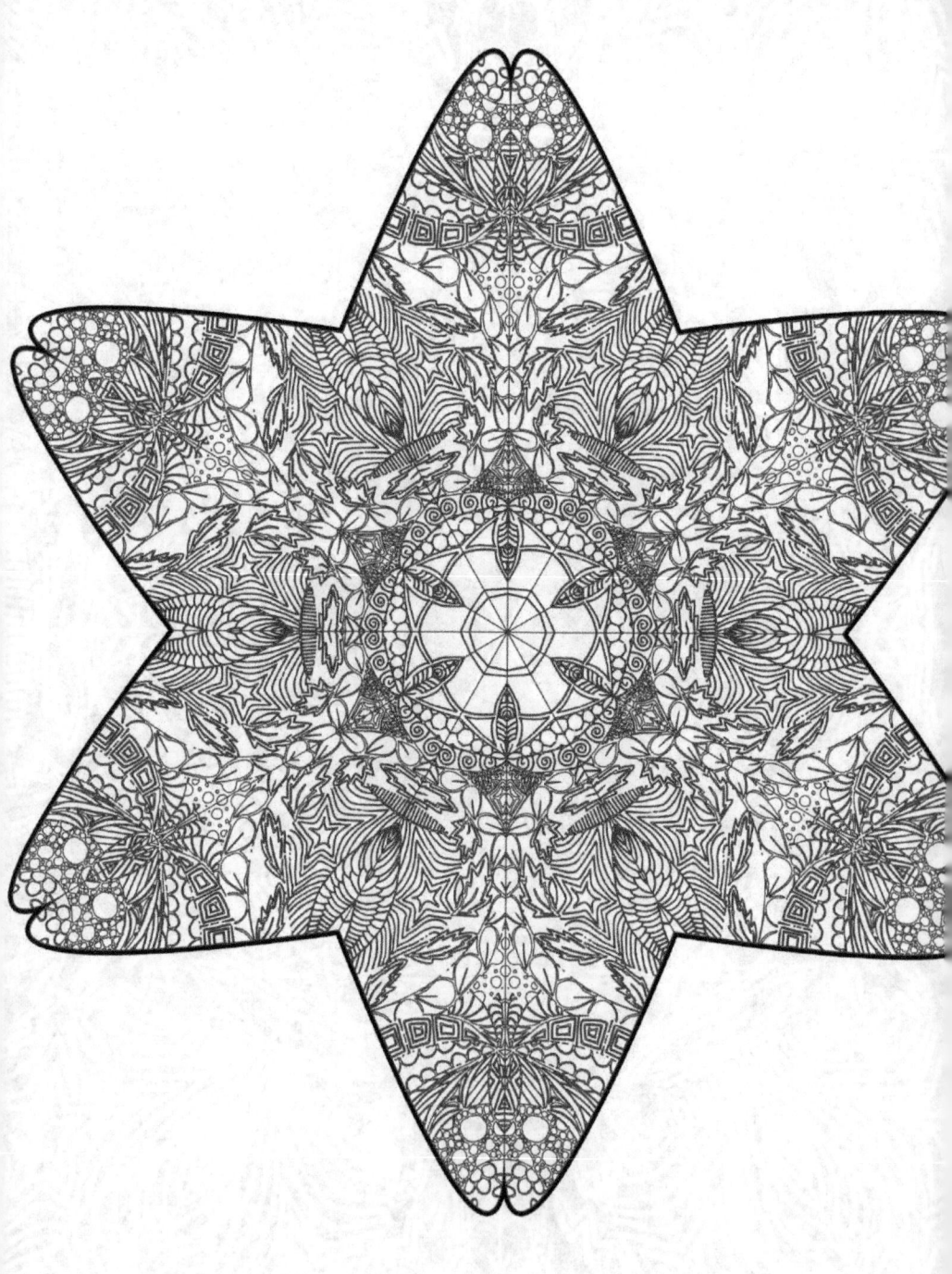

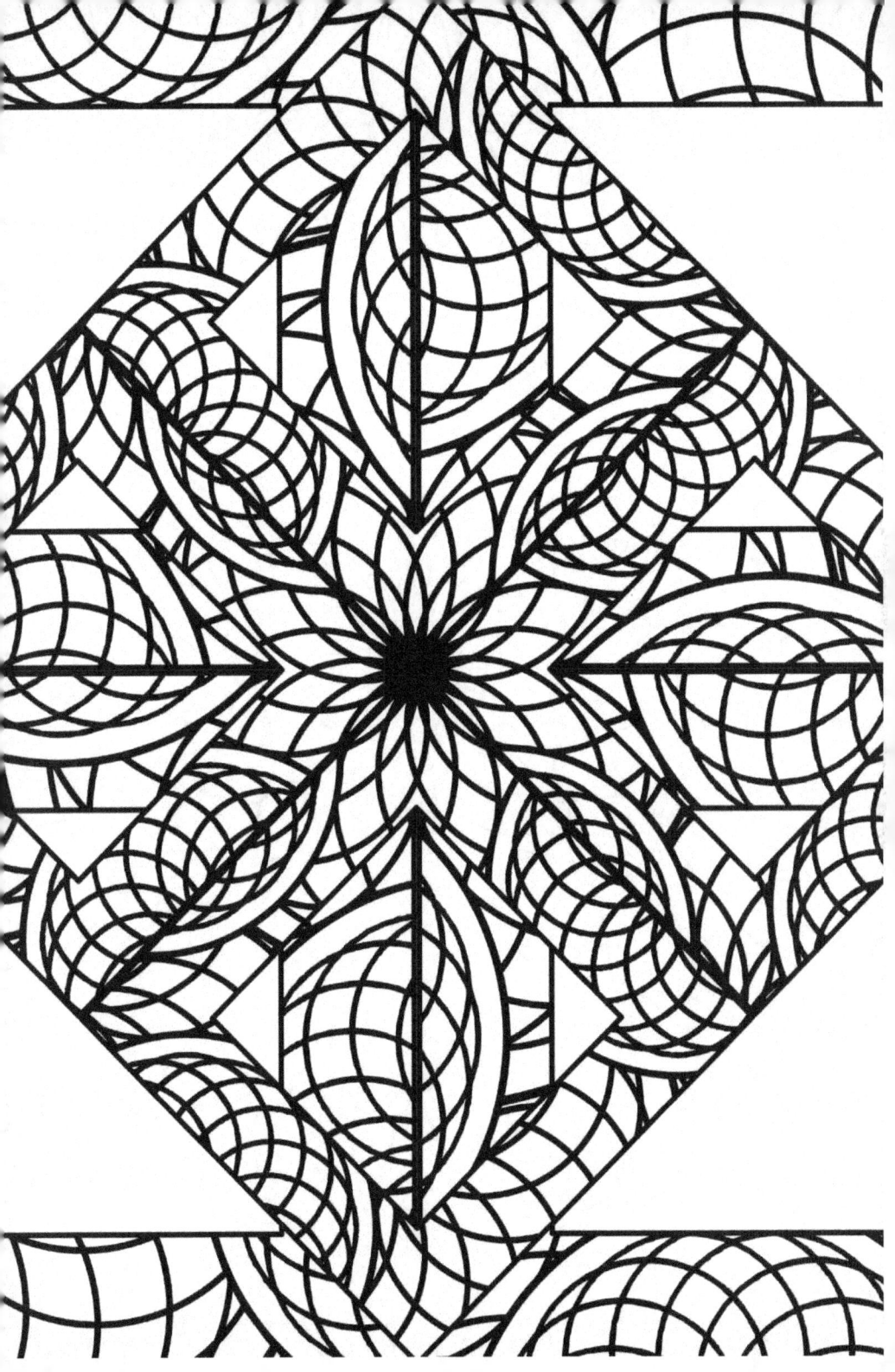

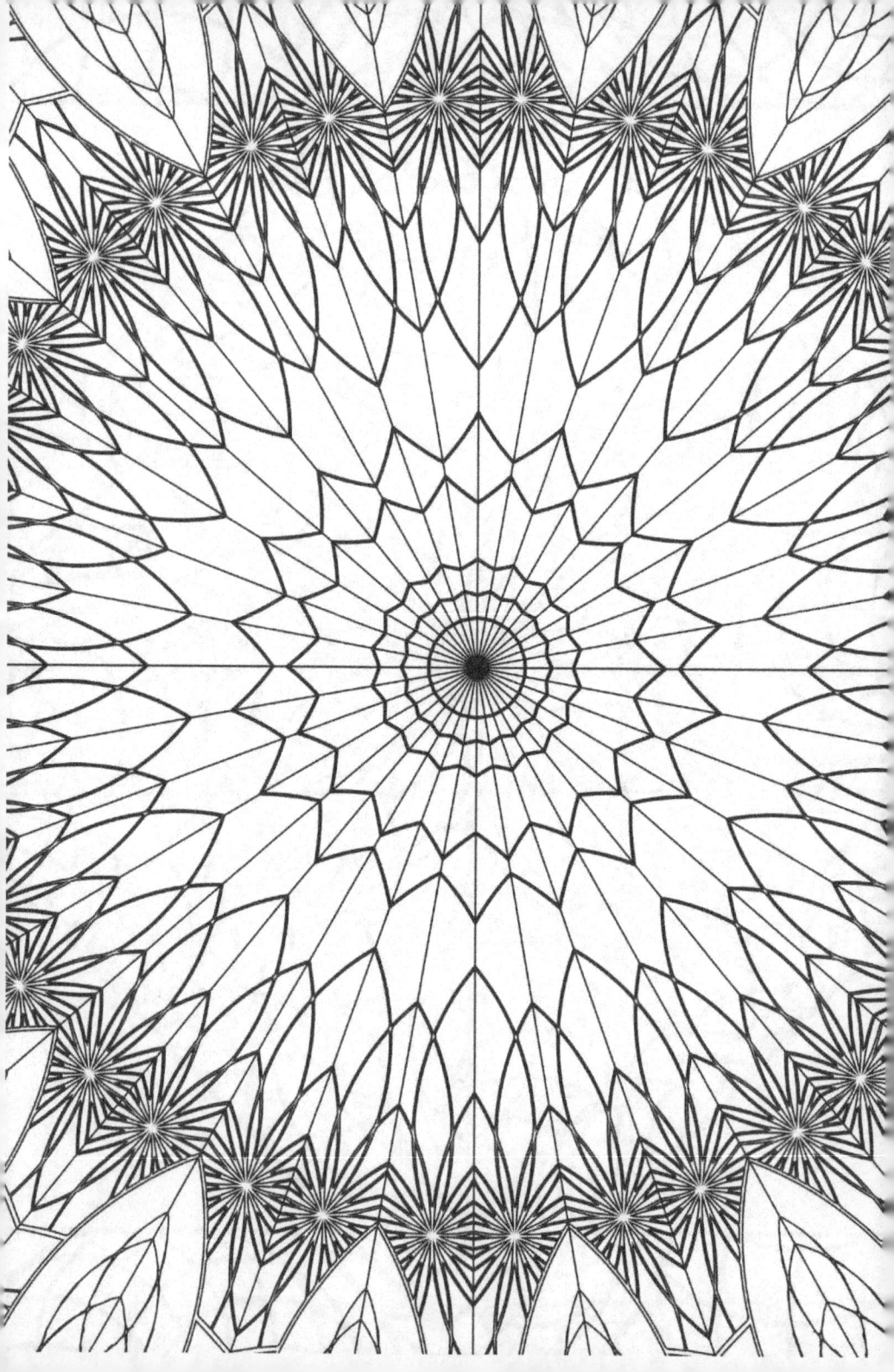

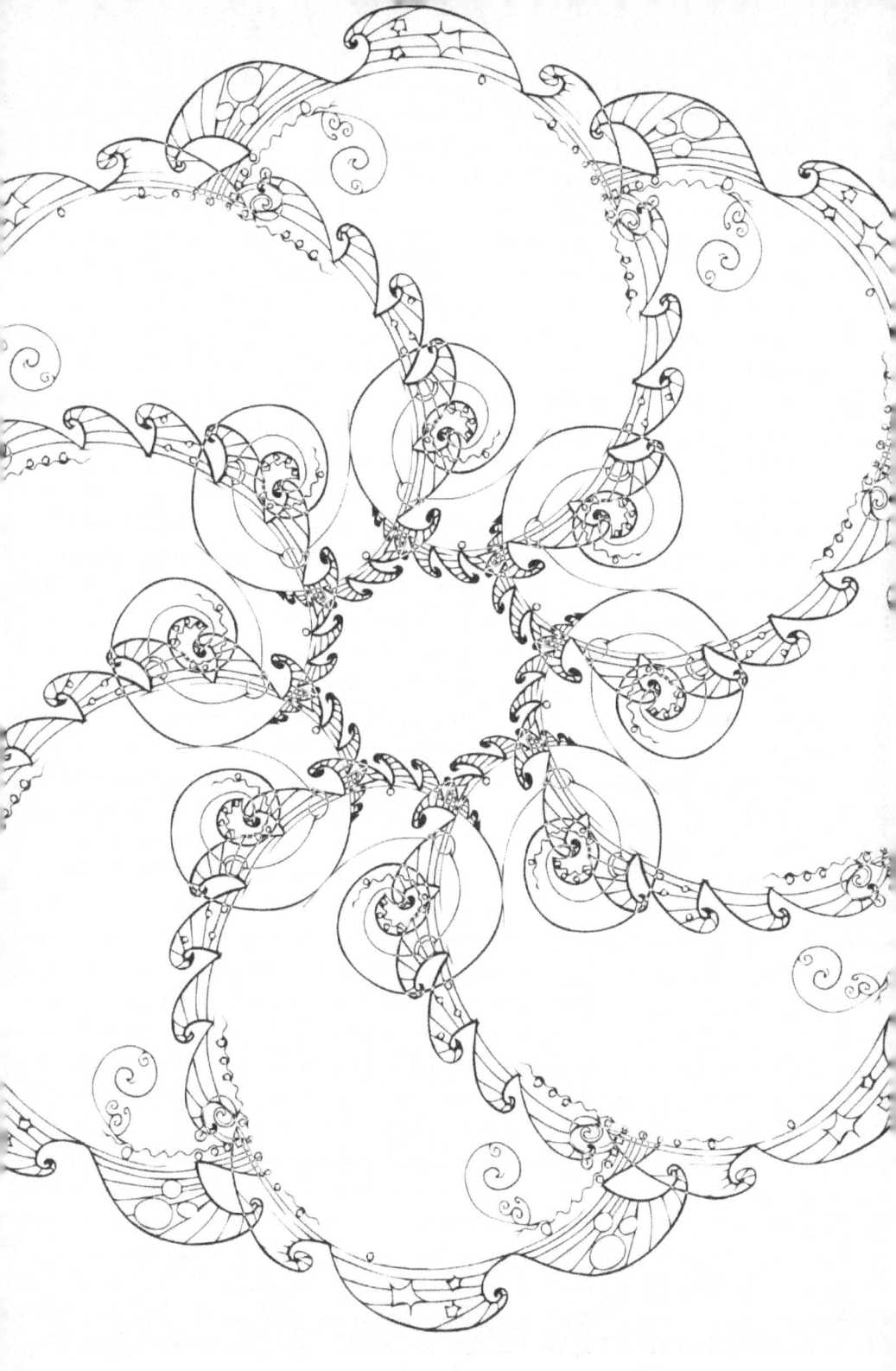

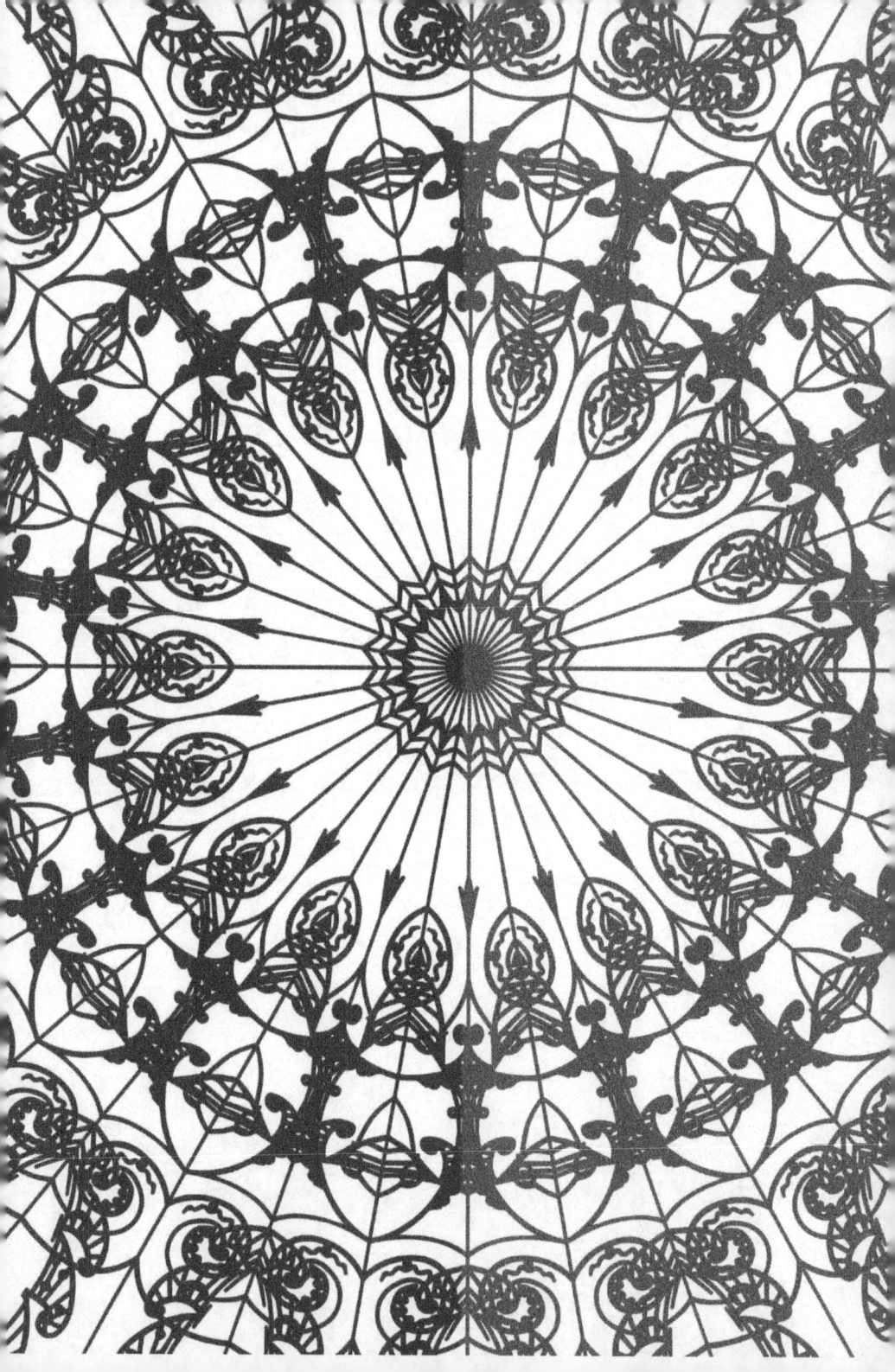

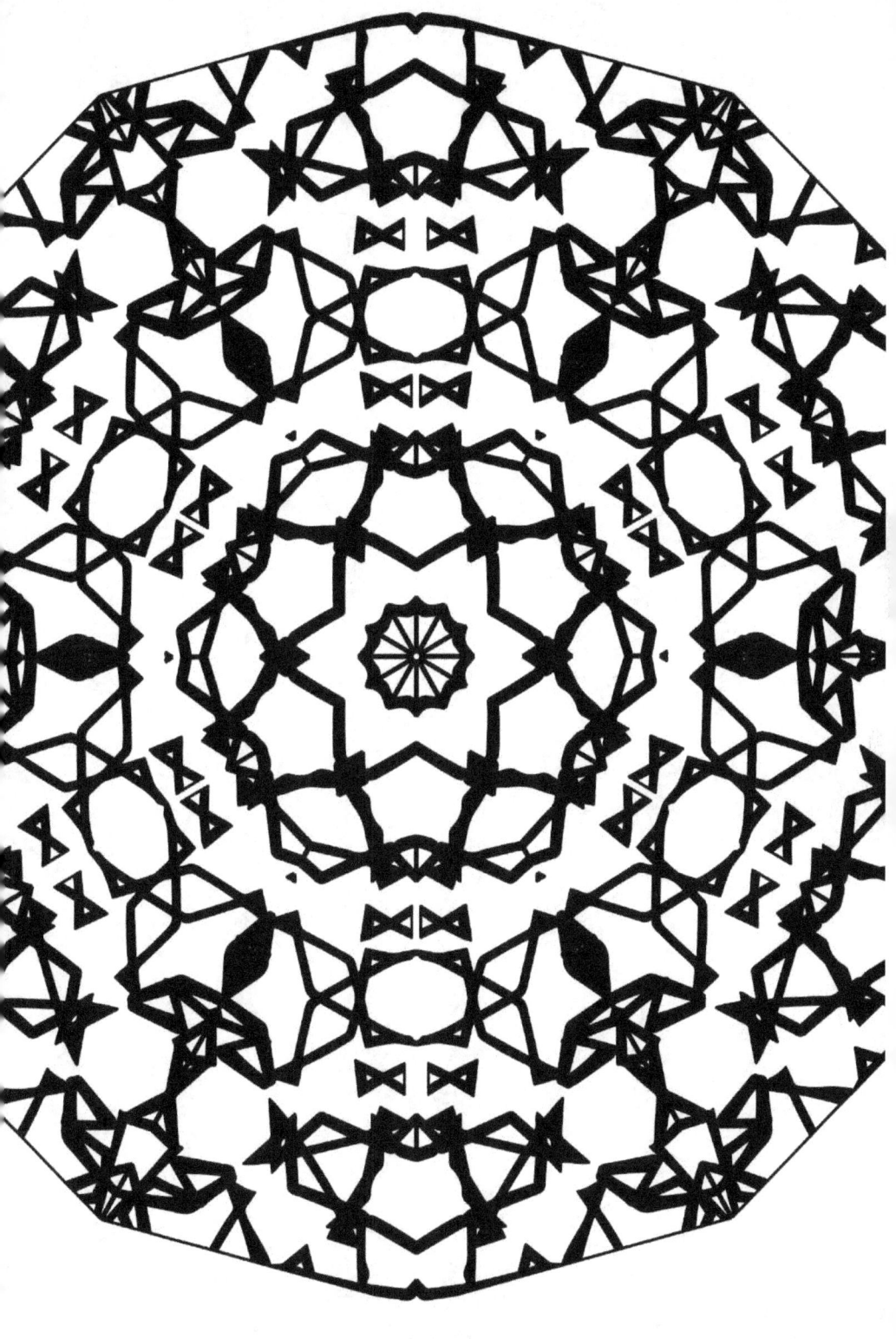

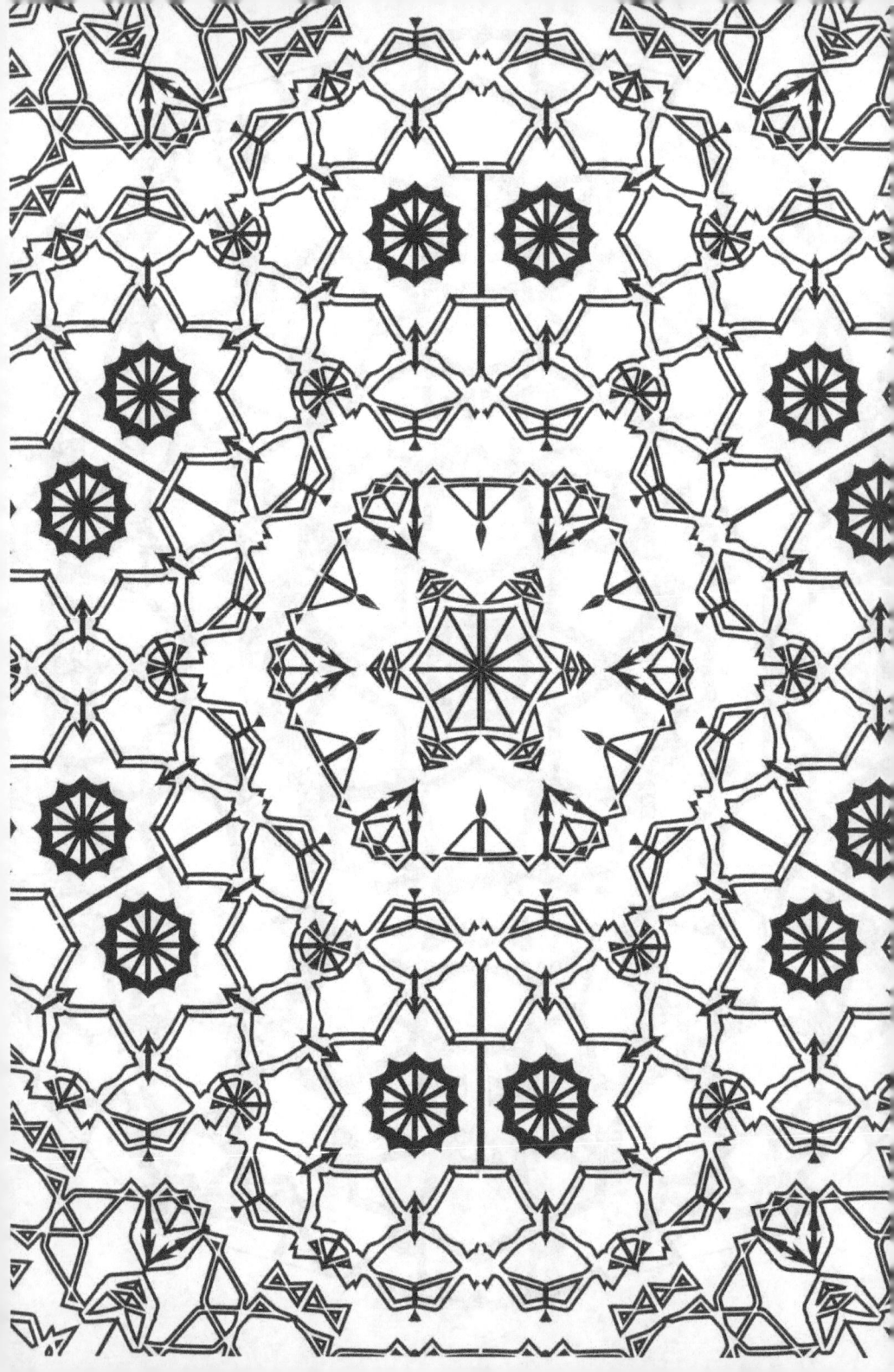

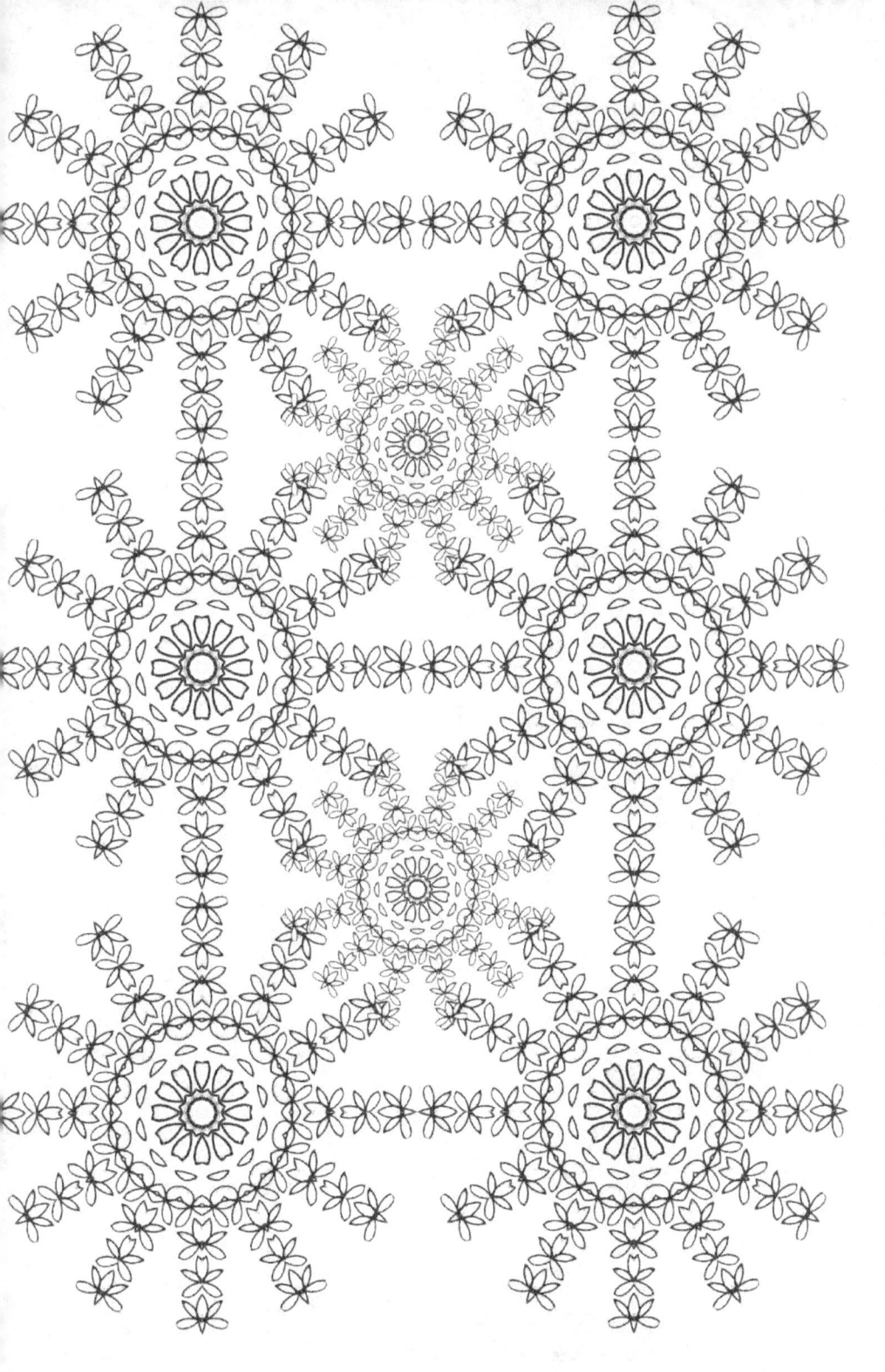

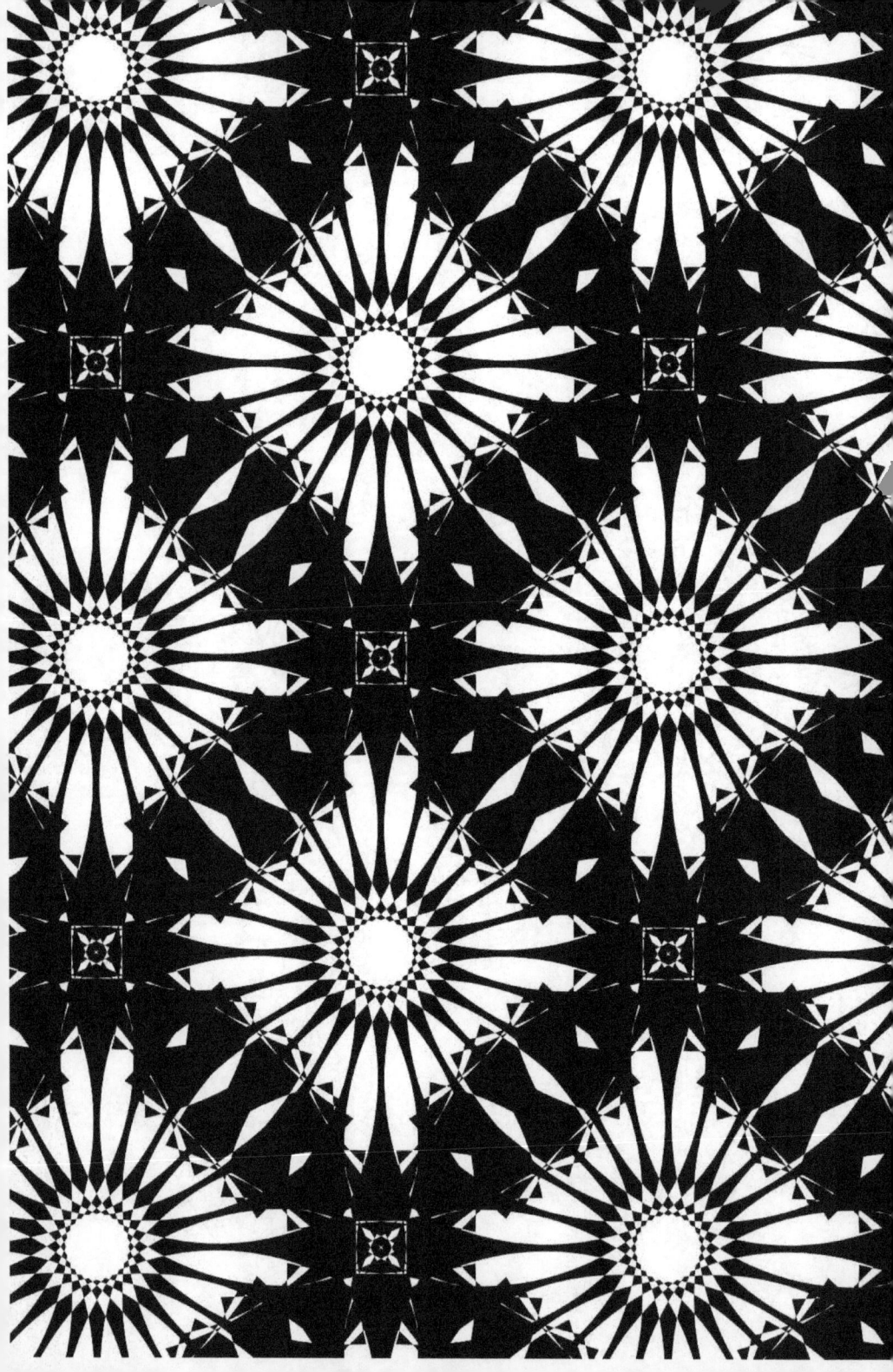

www.ingramcontent.com/pod-product-compliance
Lightning Source LLC
Chambersburg PA
CBHW061230180526
45170CB00003B/1228